date
talk

DateTalk

(almost) everything you need to know
about relationships, dating, and sex

wolfgang eckleben

To Love Well is to Live Well

AN EVERY NATION LONDON PUBLICATION

188 Hammersmith Road, W6 7DJ, United Kingdom

www.everynation.london

www.wolfinlondon.com

CONTENTS

FOREWORD

By Alison Eckleben, who dated Wolfi in their teenage years...

Well, what can I say: 25 years of marriage that genuinely seems to get better with each passing year. In my opinion, I have the best husband in the whole world. He is definitely the more magnanimous and adventurous one in our relationship, which contributes to us not settling or ending up in stalemate for very long. He has taught me to love better, and to love well.

But it didn't start out this way. We began dating in high school and did not have any dating guidelines to follow except that we both came from pretty stable family backgrounds and were fairly decent people, so initially everything ran smoothly. As we soon found out, this was not enough to develop a mutually fulfilling, healthy relationship. In fact, it quickly became dysfunctional with loads of damage from both sides. Wolfi often says: 'I was probably the world's most useless boyfriend ever!' – and he was in so many ways. I allowed him to break my heart by his actions and choices, which in turn determined how I lived my life. My early twenties were miserable and I lived life in a very small and passive way.

The game changer was us both encountering biblical truth about relationships from God's perspective. What

I love about my husband is that when he has a revelation of truth, he will consistently apply the discovered principle until he has mastered it. Not only will he do this for himself, but he is passionate about teaching these principles to others too. Hence the writing of this book. I am confident that if you apply the principles discovered in this book, you will have a better chance of experiencing a healthy relationship that honours both God and your partner. As Wolfi himself often says, 'You can either learn from experience or learn from those who have been through the experience'. My hope is that you will heed his advice and learn from what transcended out of our bad experience of doing relationships.

He is certainly one of the most authentic people I know, and lives what he teaches. My hero for sure!

Alison Eckleben
London, UK

A BRIEF GUIDE TO THE DATETALK JOURNEY

Chapter 1: We all need help

Because without love, we are nothing.

Chapter 2: Decide your guide

Because there is a Manual, and each of us needs to decide who and what will guide us on this exciting but often confusing relationship journey.

Chapter 3: I'll have a whole one please

Because the best preparation you can make for a future fulfilled relationship is an understanding and commitment to personal wholeness.

Chapter 4: Understanding the opposite sex

Because we are different, and to be a lover, you have to be a learner.

Chapter 5: Lessons from lovers' lane

Because there are always good and bad ways of doing things. Knowing what to avoid will save you much heartache, because an unwise dating journey often ends in a ditch, or at least a dead end.

Chapter 6: SexTalk

Because our sexuality is a part of every one of us. Straight talk about the myths, the Manual, and the mysteries of sex, and the one most important thing that you need to know about sex.

Chapter 7: The HighWay

Because there is a better way to do relationships than just going with the cultural flow. We look at the promise, the code, and the journey that will take you to your destination of a healthy fulfilled relationship.

Chapter 8: Recalculating your way forward

Because there is always hope and a way back to The Way.

Chapter One

WE ALL NEED HELP

When it comes to relationships, we all need help. Some of us need a lot. I certainly did.

Like the young guy who takes a girl out on a first date. At the end of a great evening he walks her home, and standing on the porch at the front door, he decides to try for what he has been thinking about most of the evening. With an air of confidence, he leans with his hand against the wall and, smiling, says to her, "Hey, how about a goodnight kiss?" Horrified, she replies, "Are you crazy? My parents will see us!" "Oh come on! It's late. Who's going to see us?" "No, please. Can you imagine if we get caught?" "Oh come on, there's nobody around, they're all sleeping!" "No way! What if my parents are awake?" "Oh please, please, I like you so much!" "No, no, and no. I like you too, but I just can't. Not now!" "Oh yes, you can. Please?" "NO, no. I just can't." "Pleeeeease?..."

Out of the blue, the porch light goes on, and the girl's sister shows up in her pyjamas, hair all in a mess, and, in a sleepy voice, says: "Dad says to go ahead and give him a kiss. Or I can do it. Or if need be, he'll come down himself and do it. But for crying out loud tell him to take his hand off the intercom button!"[1]

There are so many things that can seem to go wrong, and if we are honest, we need all the help we can get to do relationships well.

We are created for love and relationship. And attraction. And passion. And sex. And marriage. Unfortunately, most of us simply stumble along this road driven by our passions and longings, hoping to somehow fall in love and end up living happily forever after with Mr or Mrs Right. Besides our internal struggles, there are so many external pressures in our uber-sexualised do-it-if-you-like-it culture which, for the most part, is itself quite obviously confused and doesn't exactly have a track record of doing relationships well.

As I look back on my own life in the area of relationships, I see that I needed help. Loads of it. I was possibly the most clueless and useless boyfriend any girl ever had, and my wife Ali will confirm that!

I was sincere but discovered that sincerity alone was not enough. It's possible to be very sincere and yet be very sincerely wrong. Good intentions are a good start, but without adding wisdom and skills they are rarely enough to guarantee success in anything.

I had no clue how to relate to women. I didn't know what to do with the emotional feelings and sexual passions I had. I didn't know what it meant to be a real man, nor that there was any difference between being a male, or being a man. I had no positive role models to follow. Until well into my university years, I don't recall anyone ever speaking to me in any helpful way about the birds and the bees and how to treat a woman and process my feelings. I didn't grow up in a Christian home and the bit I heard from the church I was exposed to was nothing more than a vague bunch of warnings and "don'ts", without any "whys" and "hows" to help me actually do what I was being told was right. I did want a relationship, but I desperately needed help. I needed someone to help me translate my desires and passions into fulfilling relationships and to teach me what it means to love well. I needed someone to be straight with me.

They say that growth only begins when you start to know what you don't know because only then are you ready to learn. I sure had a lot to learn, and DateTalk is a collection of truth and wisdom that I discovered on my own relationship journey, and from walking with countless young people as a friend, counsellor, and pastor.

This may be a good moment to pause and admit to yourself: "I also need help."

You will notice that I am a convinced believer in Jesus, and I do bring God into the picture quite frequently throughout DateTalk. There are many reasons for this, which will come up along the way. My aim, though, is not to persuade you to believe the same things that I do on matters of faith. It is rather to share some truths that are helpful for anyone who wants to learn to build healthy relationships. So no matter what you believe right now, please keep reading, and I hope that you will find something to help you too.

In all that I have been privileged to do and be a part of in my life, I have come to realise one very significant thing: Relationships affect every area of our lives. No matter what great things we think we have accomplished (or not), and no matter what success we have had (or not), without love we are nothing. Without love, we multiply whatever we have with zero and get zero. Zilch. Nothing.

A person without love is nothing.

A church without love is nothing.

A Christian without love is nothing.

A life without love is nothing.

Without love we are nothing

There is a lot at stake, and that's why I am passionate about sharing the truth and wisdom in DateTalk with you. I believe that to love well is to live well. When you get relationships right, everything else in your life will be a whole lot richer. Every area of our lives is affected by our relationships, and relational health and maturity are vital ingredients of every person's growth. Growing in love is the greatest growing you can do in your life. No matter what you do in life, your relationships and the way you conduct them will always be a major part of your story. Sadly many people never fulfil their potential in life simply because messy relationships have tripped them up along the way. Even sadder is the fact that many people won't experience the great joy of a healthy, happy relationship because they simply never found the help they needed to make it work.

Unfortunately, for too many people, the words "relationship" and "fulfilled" do not fit well together, and this may also be the case for you. I realise that as you read this you may well be carrying hurts from past or even present broken relationships. Perhaps you have been divorced, separated, widowed, or painfully dumped. Perhaps you have been rejected, neglected, abused, used, abandoned, cheated on … and you are still hurting. Maybe you are single and waiting and finding the timing very difficult. Maybe you have been waiting a long time, and hope deferred is making your heart sick.[2] You may be feeling very lonely and without hope for a better future.

If what you read here brings past or present hurts to the surface, then I pray that DateTalk will bring healing and restore hope to you about your future. The fact is that in order to move forward you will have to find healing from the hurts and disappointments that you carry from your past. I am convinced that for most people the greatest obstacles to future fulfilment are actually what lie behind them, not ahead. It often takes more faith to let go and move on from what's behind you, than to move forward to what's ahead for you.

However badly you may have messed up in your past, please know and believe that God is the great restorer. If you want to know God's heart towards those who have messed up in relationships, just take a look at how Jesus interacted with the Samaritan woman who had had five husbands and was now living with another man.[3] Or the woman brought to him after she had been caught in the act of adultery.[4] In both cases, he was fully aware of their past, but more concerned about leading them into a better future.

Jesus didn't come to judge us, but to fix us. He is the God of second chances. And third and fourth and fifth chances, and even the seventy times seven chances! He is the lover of all lovers. He doesn't just have love, he is love. He has a future for you and he wants you to know the way to your good future filled with his blessing and hope and healthy relationships. And if the waiting is hurtful, difficult, painful or confusing, then I trust that you will see a ray of hope at the end of the tunnel and be encouraged.

I have had the privilege of presenting DateTalk as a seminar on many occasions and places around the world, and also as a series on the TBN UK television show, "The Art of Loving Well" which has aired in Europe and Africa. Sharing across these cultural divides has confirmed to me that the basic needs and principles of relationships are the same for every person everywhere, whether you live in Asia or America, in London or at the foot of the beautiful Alps in Austria.

Many couples have embraced the truths of DateTalk, and I have later had the privilege and joy of standing with them at the altar as they have made their vows. Others, through these same teachings, have found themselves needing to look at their lives and choices more carefully; to wait, to reconsider; to count the cost of commitment, and to ask each other whether this is really what both want for their lives at this time. It is surely better to be talking about these things earlier, rather than regret talking about them later.

We all have our own love story or stories. What's yours?

Pause here and take a moment to reflect back a bit on your own love story:

- What crushes have you had?
- Who was your first love?
- How was your heart broken?
- Who rejected you?
- What fantasies play out in your imagination?
- What sexual experiences have you had?
- What do you regret?

Of course, you may be reading this and have never yet dated or been in a serious romantic relationship. That's fantastic, because getting your thinking right before you start anything is always easier than trying to fix things later. I hope that DateTalk will be a part of preparing you for an exciting future relationship.

By the way, I have intentionally not filled this book with other people's stories, or even my own stories, because each of us is unique and it is so easy, and often dangerous, to compare our story to others. Instead, DateTalk focuses on principles and truths that will help you navigate your own unique, exciting and often confusing relationship journey.

Of course, I am very aware that there is so much more to say about relationships than can be covered here. Nevertheless, I pray that DateTalk will be a catalyst to launch you into a new approach to relationships, and I am excited to see what the great Match-Maker will do in your life!

The DateTalk Truth:

Everyone needs help to do relationships well

Pause to think and talk about it:

- What one thing did you find most helpful or insightful in this chapter?

- Revisit the "what's your love story" part of the chapter and consider whether there are still areas of hurt in your life. Consider finding a trusted friend and share your experiences with them. As you continue reading DateTalk I also trust that it will help you find healing and hope.

- What is one thing that you will apply to your own relationship journey from this chapter?

Chapter Two

DECIDE YOUR GUIDE

There is a lot of advice out there about love, dating and relationships. I love the wisdom of these five to ten-year-old kids who were asked the following questions:

What is the proper age to get married? *"At 84, because at that age, you don't have to work anymore, and you can spend all your time loving each other."* Judy, age 8. *"Once I'm done with kindergarten, I'm going to find me a wife!"* Tom, age 5.

Another question: What do most people do on a date? *"On the first date, they just tell each other lies, and that usually gets them interested enough to go for a second date."* Mike, age 10.

Then a question about the great debate: Is it better to be single or married? *"It's better for girls to be single but not for boys. Boys need someone to clean up after them."* Lynette, age 9. *"It gives me a headache to think about that stuff. I'm just a kid. I don't need that kind of trouble!"* Kenny, age 7.[6]

We don't know whether Mike, Lynette and Kenny pursued careers in relationship counselling in their later years! The truth is that not all advice is equal and not all is helpful. Much relationship advice has more to do with lust than love. Too much advice is about laws and rules and don'ts, without enough emphasis on the dos and the hows and the whys.

We need a more reliable source of help. As for any product, I believe that the most reliable source of advice and instruction is the manual. The word *manual* literally means *the mind of the manufacturer giving instructions on the use of a product*. If you want the best out of any product, study the manual. Often we don't get the most use out of a product because we simply have not followed the manual. As a result, we may under-utilise, misuse or even destroy the product in our ignorance or pride.

Have you heard the story Jesus told about a prodigal son?[7] That son started out demanding "Father give me" until his frustrations and failures got him to a place of asking "Father make me". How many of us have done the same? At some point in life, you have to get over your pride and look for help. From my own painful experience let me encourage you to make this decision sooner rather than later. There are two ways to learn: either by experience or from someone who has had the experience.

I believe that the Bible is the Maker's manual for living life to the full. If you want the best out of this thing called life and relationships, try doing it according to this Manual. Maybe you don't personally believe in God and have all sorts of questions about the Bible, but let me encourage, even challenge you to read what the God of the Bible says about you and see if that might ring true. I guarantee that by following the principles of this Manual will greatly improve your living and your loving. Neither the Bible, nor DateTalk is about a bunch of rules, but rather about a way to do relationships better. Jesus called himself "The Way", and he invites you to follow him to find real life and fulfilment in every area, including your relationships.

We see the wisdom of the Manual when Jesus was once asked a tricky relationship question by the religious leaders of the time:

> [8]*Some Pharisees came and tried to trap him with this question:*
>
> *"Should a man be allowed to divorce his wife for just any reason?"*

Divorce was a controversial and difficult issue of that day. But what relationship questions would people want to ask him if he were in your city, school or on your campus today?

What relationship question would you like to ask him? How about:

- Jesus, how far is too far?
- Jesus, do you have any tips for online dating?
- Jesus, what's the big deal with sex before marriage?
- Jesus, how will I know when I have met Mr. or Mrs. Right?
- Jesus, what about same-sex marriage?
- Jesus, what about masturbation?
- Jesus, I think I'm gay. What do I do about my same-sex attraction?
- Jesus, is my porn habit really a problem?

- Jesus, is it a good idea for a non-Christian to date/ marry a Christian?
- Jesus, how do I move on after I have been cheated on?
- Jesus, would you recommend I read 50 shades of Grey, or watch Game of Thrones?
- Jesus, can you help me understand men/women better?!

PAUSE: What are your one or two big relationship questions?

So back to the question Jesus was asked.

Divorce was a big deal then, and even though many play it down today, it's still a pretty big deal especially when it affects you personally. Sadly some relationships do end, even despite the best efforts of everyone involved. You may have personally experienced this either directly or indirectly with friends or your parents. As with most big issues it's easy to have a lot of opinions and judgements until you actually face the issue yourself.

One of the reasons that the Pharisee's question was tricky that day was not just because they wanted to get Jesus on the wrong side of the law, but because King Herod had recently had John the Baptist's head chopped off because of the stand he took on Herod divorcing his wife. Now the Pharisees wanted to get Jesus into trouble whichever way he answered this question.

WARNING: The way you answer questions could get you your head chopped off! Here's a tip to help you to engage well when asked a difficult question: Before answering, make sure that you understand what the real question is. In most cases when someone asks you a personal question, a straight yes or no is not the best answer, because you generally do not yet understand the *why* of the question posed. The best answer to most questions is usually a clarifying question, like: "Why do you ask that question?" Then make sure that you first listen to understand, not just to reply. When you are interested in what others think, they may be interested in what you think. Sadly most of us tend to answer before we understand the real question, so learn to listen and understand before you reply. By the way, this approach will also hugely help you in every relationship that you have, not just the romantic kind.

OK, that was just for free. Now let's have a look at how Jesus answers this particular relationship question.

> [9]"Haven't you read, he (Jesus) replied, "that at the beginning the Creator 'made them male and female', and said, 'for this reason a man will leave his father and mother and be united/joined to his wife, and the two will become one flesh'? So they are no longer two, but one. Therefore what God has joined together, let man not separate."

To answer the question, Jesus – master of relationships if ever there was one – does something remarkable. He doesn't answer the question directly, but rather refers the questioners back to God's original intent and design for relationships by quoting from the beginning of the book of beginnings - Genesis chapters one and two. He reminds them of the Maker's original blueprint for relationships, starting his answer like this:

"Haven't you read that at the beginning"

Jesus points them to a source for the answer to their question. You see, the most effective way to identify a flaw or counterfeit is to compare it to the original. By studying and knowing the Maker's original masterplan and design, we can find our answers to our relationship questions. When you feel you've lost your way, remember this: God still has the original plan on file!

There may be a whole lot of variations and opinions about relationships and how they could and should work in our culture and generation right now, but Jesus points us back to the original plan, and his answer is a clear reminder of the foundational truths about us and relationships.

So where do you turn for help and guidance? There is so much advice and information coming at us through magazines and books and TV shows and movies and through all the ever-growing portals of the world wide web. Culture invites and entices you to conform to its image, promising acceptance and happiness if you will just walk in its ways. In the midst of this noise, I believe that God still holds up his original blueprint, inviting you to walk in his ways and discover the real path to life and fulfilled relationships.

I propose to you that your Maker who knows you best is your most reliable helper and guide. Jesus promised that "the truth will set you free."[10] Truth is not just the law sprinkled with a bit of grace. Truth is a Person. Jesus. He said, "I am the truth."[11] His truth is not a bunch of laws and rules and instructions, but a great invitation to life in all its fullness. I realise that obedience is close to a swear word in most of our culture, where we would rather go with whatever *feels* right than to consider what *is* right and best. In the wisdom book of Proverbs we read another invitation:

> *My child, pay attention to what I say. Listen carefully to my words. Don't lose sight of them. Let them penetrate deep into your heart, for they bring life to those who find them.*[12]

They will bring life to those who find them. I am convinced that God's will is good and perfect and best for you. I want to encourage you to decide to trust his truth as your guide, believing that his words and wisdom will lead you to life when you find and follow them.

"the Creator made them"

This reminds you that you were created in God's image, as was every other person alive. No one is simply an accident or a product of evolution, but a unique, special creation. The Apostle Paul, writing to the Ephesians,[13] reminds us that we are all God's "created masterpieces". The prophet Jeremiah also tells us that "Before you were knitted together in your mother's womb, God knew you."[14] You were made in heaven! You were not an accident, but a specially planned and wanted child of God your Father.

In considering how God has created us, the psalmist David declares that we are "fearfully and wonderfully made!"[15] That's you - created by God for his pleasure and purposes, and this is the most important source of your identity and value. More than knowing and believing this for yourself, you also need to know and believe this for every single other person. Recognise that everybody is special to somebody. Only then will you treat other people as valuable in your relationships. We love well when we treat others as special, belonging to God, and ourselves as the same.

"them"

God started with two single people. This is where we start. You were born as a separate individual, not joined to someone else. That's why the best place to start preparing for a future fulfilled relationship is with yourself, and we will look at this in more detail in chapter two, titled "I'll have a whole one please".

"male and female"

He made them different: male and female. Have you noticed that they are different? (If you haven't, get someone to check your pulse!) Women may not really be from Venus nor men from Mars[16], but it sure often feels like it! Understanding the opposite sex and the other is a critical part of forming healthy relationships. We look at this important aspect in detail in chapter three, "Understanding the opposite sex". That's going to be fun, and oh so important.

"therefore"

This is an important word in the Manual; it means "because of what's just been said or explained". So whenever you read this, make sure you understand what it is referring to. In Jesus' response here, he is connecting the "He created them male and female" in Genesis chapter one to the "man and wife" marriage picture in Genesis chapter two. God's original plan included man and wife joined in marriage.

"a man will"

Notice that the Manual says that they were created "male and female" but it is a "man" who is ready to get married. It was a huge challenge to me to realise that there was a big difference between being male and being a man. Being a male is a matter of birth, but becoming a man is a matter of maturity. Being a female is a matter of birth, but becoming a woman is a matter of maturity. A male and female may be able to have sex, but it takes a man and a woman to make a marriage work and raise children.

Being a male is a matter of birth, but becoming a man is a matter of maturity

"leave his father and mother and be joined to his wife"

This reminds us that there is always something or someone to leave before you can be truly joined to another. We all come into our present with some baggage from our past. You have to *leave* well before you can *cleave* well. The way you leave determines the way you will enter; the way you leave one relationship is the way you will enter the next. The way you deal with your past will definitely influence your future. To love well requires us to leave childish ways behind, and keep growing in maturity.

"the two will become one"

The Maker made male and female with the potential to become one. We were created for relationship. We are wired for relationship. A "one" relationship is not a casual relationship, but a committed "until death parts us" covenant relationship. The desires you have for companionship and a committed relationship with someone of the opposite sex are in perfect agreement with your Divine design.

"one flesh"

This includes your sexuality. God created us as sexual beings. Our sexual desires are strong reminders that we were made for relationship. We all need loads of help to figure this out and get the most out of this amazing feature of the product, but you will need a bit of patience until chapter six.

"what God joins together"

God your creator is in the joining together business. He is not only your Maker but also the great Matchmaker! Throughout this book, I want to continually encourage you to trust him, because he is faithful and able. I want to encourage you to trust him not just in the "who you will join", but also in the "how you will go about joining", or pursuing and doing relationships.

"let not man separate"

While we are created for relationship and are drawn to relationships, and God does join us together in relationships, the reality is that we all have stuff and tendencies in our lives that tend to mess up and destroy the very relationships that we so desperately want and enjoy. Soon after Adam and Eve had become one and were "naked and unashamed" with each other, they were hiding from each other and from God behind fig leaves, blaming each other for what went wrong. All across the earth sincere people are falling in love and falling out of love, getting married and getting divorced, leaving broken hearts, broken hopes and broken families in the wake of their attempts to get relationships right.

So that was Jesus' answer to the relationship question they asked him to try to trick him. His answer lays a framework for the answer to all our own relationship questions, and my hope is that DateTalk will lay a solid foundation of wisdom and truth to help you navigate your own relationship journey in a more safe and fulfilling way.

This journey though, starts with you, and that is what the next chapter is about.

The DateTalk Truth:

The Manual is your most reliable guide in all of life

Pause to think and talk it through:

- Consider: What sources have most influenced your thinking and approach to relationships?

- Which part of Jesus' answer to the Pharisees do you find most difficult to accept for yourself, and why?

- What is one thing that you will apply to your own relationship journey from this chapter?

Chapter Three

I'LL HAVE A WHOLE ONE PLEASE

Rick Warren's bestselling book, The Purpose Driven Life, starts like this: "It's not about you.[17]"

When it comes to preparing for relationships though, it is *first* about you. It *starts* with you. Andy Stanley once asked this powerful question to not-yet-marrieds: *"Are you the one that the one you are looking for is looking for?"* Did you get that? Perhaps you need to read that question again. Maybe you do feel ready for a relationship, and I in no way want to tell you that you are not ready. What I do want to do in this chapter is to help you think more clearly about "you", and I want to show you that the very best preparation you can make for a future fulfilled relationship is a commitment to keep developing your personal wholeness.

Just as much as you are looking for someone, I want to remind you that the someone you are looking for, is also looking for someone. When they do bump into you, what will they find? Will you be the one that the one you are looking for is looking for? Are you becoming that one? So we start with you because right now the only one you can do anything about is you. You have no control over anyone else. In fact, once you are married, you will still be the only one you can do something about as you continue to commit to being the spouse your marriage needs in order to flourish, rather than trying to get your spouse to change. That, by the way, is a very bad idea - as many a spouse has found out!

Don't ever believe that marriage will complete you. At its best, it will only complement you.

It is said that the biggest room for improvement is right in our own house. While we are looking out of the window longing to find the one we are looking for, we must also look in the mirror and consider our own personal growth journey.

Going back to the prodigal son Jesus spoke about in his famous parable, our journeys often start with "give me", but at some point we need to say, "Father, make me. Help me to be ready for all you have for me." Too often when it comes to our desire for a relationship our cry is, "Father, give me one" when it should be "Father, make me *one*" – help me to get ready for a relationship. Once the prodigal son was committed to the "make me" process, he got all that he desired, and so much more. I pray that it will be the same for you. This chapter is about the "make me" part of the journey.

The Manual says that "the two will become one." But how does a one and a one make a one? I figured that since God started with "be fruitful and multiply", he is a God of multiplication, and that the way to satisfy this equation is that it takes a whole one times a whole one to make a whole one. So to get a whole one relationship, you need to put two whole ones together. No other options give a whole one result. For example, a ½ × 1 results in a ½. Similarly, a ½ × ½ results in a ¼, etc. The point is simply this: if you want the best out of a relationship, you need two whole ones getting together, and from this, we can draw two conclusions:

Firstly: To be ready for a relationship, you must commit to becoming and being a whole one.

Secondly: If you're looking for a partner, look for a whole one. If you are choosing or putting in an order, say: "I'll have a whole one please!" If you are joining yourself to someone in a relationship, make sure you join yourself to a whole one.

Now, what does a "whole one" look like? Well, it definitely doesn't mean perfection. If it did then none of us would be candidates for a healthy relationship because the last time I checked we were all still a work in progress. A successful marriage relationship is not about two perfect people living happily ever after.

If you are looking for perfection, I am afraid you will need to commit yourself to celibacy! Adam was the last man to ever see a perfect woman, and Eve was the last woman to ever see a perfect man. They sinned, and since then, it's been about two imperfect people loving each other with God's help. I know that may not sound very inspiring or romantic, but that's the way it is.

Wholeness is about maturity, and being in a process of maturing. I suggest that a whole person is one who can confidently make the following statements about themselves, and who is growing in living these out at the core of their being.

I am a whole one when I can confidently say:

I have a life

I am unique

I am loved

I am a man/woman

I am valuable

I have left

I am ready for *us*

Let's have a look at each of these "I am/I have" statements now.

I HAVE A LIFE

As a whole person, you have a life, whether you have a relationship or not. You are not waiting around and looking for a life in a relationship. You have a life to deposit into a future relationship, rather than waiting for someone else to come along and give you a life. You have a life, and when you do have a relationship you will have a life to share with another person.

You don't have a life when you are investing all your energy and self-esteem into getting a date or trying to get someone to have a relationship with you. You don't have a life when all your focus is on waiting to get a life through a next relationship. You don't have a life when your life's on hold while you are waiting to fall in love. You don't have a life when you are depending on another person to complete you. You don't have a life when your main goal in life is having a partner or getting married.

You have a life when you don't need somebody to be somebody. People who need other people to have a life and be whole are the most manipulated and manipulating people in the world. To need another person to give you a life is a sure way to get trapped and stay trapped in a relationship that isn't right for you.

You have a life when you don't need somebody to be somebody

To have a life means that you are growing. Not just older, but more mature. Having a life means you have friends, not just a boy or girlfriend. It means to have interests, hobbies, dreams, vision; something to live for greater than yourself. Having a life means that you are not just living to get, but living to give and be a blessing to others.

You can say, "I have a life" when getting a boyfriend or girlfriend or getting married is not your ultimate goal in life, but you have dreams and vision and a goal for your own life apart from anyone else. You have a life when you have a sense of purpose and are actively pursuing it.

So, don't look for a wife to get a life, or a man to get a life.

Can you confidently say: I have a life?

I AM UNIQUE

Oscar Wilde said: "Be yourself because everyone else is already taken."

To be unique means to know and accept that you are one of a kind. You are not truly whole until you understand and accept that there is nobody else like you. No duplicates.

There is no rival for being you. When the Maker made you, he made you unique, and then he threw the mould away and said: "I'll never make another one like this!" That's not because he didn't like what he made, but because he absolutely loves what he made. God doesn't make junk. God created you unique. There is no one like you. And he loves you as he made you. This is all true whether you believe it or not. But until you believe it, you are not whole.

The sad thing is that while we are all born originals, far too many people will die as copies. Don't live as a copy of someone else. If you're trying to be somebody else, there will always be somebody else better than you, because they're the original, and you're just the copy. Remember, a copy never has as much value as the original. People who are trying to be copies of others will always give themselves away cheaply, and then wonder why they feel used in relationships.

We are all born originals, but sadly far too many people will die as copies.

To be whole means to be free from the pressure to compare and conform. When you understand that you are unique, it sets you free from comparing and conforming and being enslaved to others. You are unique. You are different. You make the best you.

The Manual says: Don't conform to the image of this world. Don't let the world squeeze you into its mould.[18] There is always a pressure to conform to others; to be the same. We were never designed to be the same. So stop conforming.

You know you are unique when you don't need to be like anyone else to be somebody. If you still need to always be wearing the latest fashion and have the latest gadgets to feel you're somebody, then you aren't whole yet. Now, my advice is that you do keep up with fashion a bit. It may even help you! But don't be a slave to it. Don't be defined by the label on your jeans, or even worse the label on your jocks! You are not what you wear.

Stop comparing yourself to others. The Manual says that the one who compares himself to another is foolish.[19] That's a strong warning because comparison is so dangerous and enslaving. Stop comparing yourself to images pumped at you through the media. We've all done it. We look at other people's photos and posts on social media and something in us wonders why we aren't also living the perfect life everyone else seems to be living. We forget that most of what we view across the media front is photoshopped and a very carefully staged illusion. It's not real because it's not complete. No one posts their bad hair and bad breath days, yet we think we are the only ones who have them.

Beware of thinking and saying things like, "If only I was more this... or less that... or more attractive... or richer... or..."

Here's something I totally believe: *Everybody is sexy to somebody.* In your uniqueness, you are desirable and attractive to the right somebody for you. Believe that.

Everybody is sexy to somebody

You know you're whole when you can walk into a room and introduce yourself: "Hi. My name is _____. I'm the only one of my kind. Enjoy me now because you'll never meet another one like me!"

You make the best you there is. You are a whole one when you accept that and live that. When you meet someone who is obviously trying to be somebody they are not, be careful because that's a sure sign that they still have some wholeness to find before they are ready for a relationship.

I AM LOVED

One of our deepest human needs is the need to be loved, to belong, to be accepted. Now, it's relatively easy to find someone that you love, but what you really, really want to find is somebody who loves you. You want someone to love the real you. The whole you.

The problem is that we all know there is more to us than the best foot we put forward when we meet someone. There's not only our good, but also our bad and our ugly. This leaves us with a big question: If they *really* knew me, would they still love me?

The reality is there is no one on this planet who can love you like you need to be loved in order to feel truly loved. There is no man or woman who can love you like you really need to be loved. Ladies, even if you find your knight in shining armour, you will discover that his armour has some dents in it. Men, the princess you rescue may have looked stunning in her tower, but close-up you are bound to find some flaws. Like I said before: Mr. & Mrs. Perfect simply don't exist.

Many will try to find this love in bed. But sex will never say "I love you" like you need to hear it. It will never be enough. It may scratch an itch but it will never take it away. After a night of passion, both women and men still ask the other: Do you love me? Especially in our casual sex culture, sex obviously isn't that special thing reserved for someone special, so how can it then communicate anything special? That's just a start on the sex subject · there's much more to come in the following chapters...

So, where do you find that unconditional love? Let me explain this to you from my Christian faith point of view. You see, I fully believe that there is a deep desire in each of us that transcends our desire for a special person or even a spouse, and that is our desire for a relationship with our Creator God. As I read the Bible I see that God doesn't just *have* love; he *is* love. The motivation of all God did through Christ was love. For God so loved the world that he gave his only son.[20] It was because of God's great love that Christ offered up his very own life in our place for our sins on the cross. "No greater love has anyone than to lay his life down for another."[21] Jesus did this for you because of his great love for you.

When you understand the Christian faith, you know that God loves you lavishly and unconditionally and that he wants to pour his perfect love into your heart to fill you and overflow you, so that you can pour it out to others too.

When you receive this love, you can also give it to others. When the other person has this love, they can give it to you. If you haven't received this love, you can't give love. If you receive this perfect love from God – if you can confidently with faith say: "I am one loved by God" – then you can also give love to others.

The problem is that when you look for this perfect unconditional love from another person, they will never be able to fully satisfy you because they can't give you what only God can give you. As difficult as it is for some to accept, this truth also reminds us that marriage and relationship with the opposite sex are not the highest priority of life. God is. Everything starts and flows from him and his love.

I am convinced that if you don't find and accept God's love for you, then you will always have unrealistic expectations from your relationships, and this will eventually drain the life out of them. Decide today that no one will ever take God's place in your life. Know and receive his love for you. Be loved and live loved by God.

Even further, decide that you will not pursue a relationship with anyone who does not have the same desire for God's presence as you. A relationship is a very lonely place when you can't share your greatest joy with the person who's the closest to you. Wholeness is attained when God's love and presence fully satisfy you. You are only as whole as you allow yourself to be changed more and more into God's image as revealed in Jesus Christ. Learn to pursue his presence before you start to pursue a partner.

Remember, the Manual says that "In God's presence is fullness of joy".[22] It does not say "in the presence of my boyfriend/girlfriend/husband/wife is fullness of joy." If you look for fullness of joy in other places and people, you will always come away empty.

"I am one loved by God" is an amazing thing to be able to say, and it's a vital key to personal wholeness.

I AM A MAN/WOMAN

Notice I didn't say *I am a male or female*. The Manual says that we were created male and female. As I consider our human form and function, everything in our design shouts that we were made male and female to be fruitful and multiply, the two designed to fit together perfectly in passionate sexual intimacy for pleasure and for reproduction. Gender identity is a huge issue in our culture, and coming to peace about your gender is vitally important to personal wholeness. For some, and perhaps you, this is a very difficult topic, and here I simply want to raise the issue as obviously important.

If you are struggling with your gender identity, please do find somewhere safe to talk about it. Every Christian friend and every church should be a safe place for you to talk honestly and openly without feeling judged. If you don't find them understanding and helpful, please don't conclude that all Christians and churches are like that. While it is true that there are lifestyles and actions that are not possible to reconcile with what the Scriptures teach, the attitude of a Christ-follower should always be love, grace and seeking to understand and to help those struggling with any issues in life. I hope that you will find this amongst the Christians you know.

So, the Manual says, "God created them male and female," but then it says that "a man will leave his father and mother." God created him as a male, but it is a *man* who leaves his father and mother and is joined to his wife. There is a difference between being a male and being a man, and between being a female and a woman. Being a male is a matter of birth, but being a man is a matter of maturity and wholeness.

Men: don't just marry a female. Women: don't just marry a male. Yes, they may be sexy and handsome, but it takes much more than that to make a fulfilled relationship.

It takes maturity, so make sure that maturity is part of your definition of what handsome or sexy looks like.

You are whole when you are growing up in all areas of life. We will all keep growing older every day, but sadly many people won't keep growing up. Commit to continue growing up into the mature man or woman you were created to be.

I AM VALUABLE

The value you place on yourself – as a man or woman · will determine what and who you will give yourself to in life and relationships. God calls you precious, but you have to accept yourself as precious and valuable. You are the one who upholds that value. People will treat you according to the value you place on yourself.

Question: What do you expect from someone in exchange for the privilege of taking you out to dinner, holding your hand, kissing you, or having sex with you? Will it just take some flirting, some interest, some attention? Or will it take much more than that?

Ladies, consider sex as an example: What does a man need to offer you before you will sleep with him? Are those three little words, "I love you", said in the glow of some candlelight enough for you? Or maybe some flattery and flirting and attention? Is that all it takes? Or do you value yourself higher than that? I suggest you need to set the price a lot higher: set the price at nothing less than two little words, "I do". That will sort out the men from the males.

If you don't value yourself highly, you'll give yourself away cheaply, and then you'll wonder why he doesn't treat you with the value you deserve. Once you have given yourself at a certain value, it is very difficult to raise the value. Ladies, once a man has paid a low price for enjoying your body, he will treat you cheaply. You gave him what he wanted at a discount price, but I can assure you that it will cost you dearly because there is simply no way that you can separate what you do sexually from your personal sense of wholeness.

Men: What does a woman need to do to get you? Is her throwing herself at you enough? Will you take anyone who flirts with you? Anyone who is available? Offers of sex? There are many desperate and broken women who will simply want to use you and your body too. Taking up an offer of a cheap thrill will quickly devalue you too, so don't do it.

For now, make a decision that you have high value and that you don't come cheap for anybody.

Don't let anyone else determine your worth.

I HAVE LEFT

In the Manual, we read: "Therefore a man will leave his father and mother and cleave to his wife [not girlfriend!], and the two will become one flesh."[23] The way you leave is the way you will cleave. This is obviously speaking about leaving a parental relationship to enter a marital relationship, but I believe the principle also applies more broadly. It's easy to just "walk away" from past relationships, but that is not the same as to "leave". To "leave" means to un-attach, to separate, and in some cases to abandon. There are people and things you need to un-attach from and to separate from, before you are whole and ready for a relationship. The person you will get into a future relationship with does not want your old boyfriends and girlfriends and fantasies as part of the deal.

To move forward you will need to abandon some hurts and disappointments from past relationships that didn't work out. You will need to stop thinking about Handsome Harry and Sexy Suzy and your "if only" fantasies about them. You may need to go and find those old photos of past crushes and exes that you keep filed away in some secret place. Get them out, look them in the eye and say, "Goodbye. I'm leaving! I'm moving on to the new!" Then tear up that photo and chuck it. It's time to leave.

The truth is that your past has the power to keep you from your future. Don't let disappointments in your past keep you from appointments in the future. Leave them. Let them go. Get healing. Move on. The future is bright for you.

I AM READY FOR US

The Manual says that the Maker *makes all things beautiful in its time*.[24] There is a right time for everything. There is a wrong time for some things. This is also true for relationships. There is a right time for them, and there is a wrong time for them. Don't go into an exclusive relationship with someone before you are ready for that kind of intensity and commitment.

Consider that there are generally three stages in life: Me Time, Us Time, and Them Time. Me Time is when the focus is on yourself. This is a time for focussing on your personal formation, preparation and growth. It's here where you are developing your internal values, character, habits, and vision for your own life. This is when you prioritise your education and discover your interests and hobbies. It's a time for personal shaping before you join yourself to another and need to shape yourself around them.

Us Time is when you commit yourself to someone exclusively in a relationship, and getting married. The focus here is on your partner and spouse.

Them Time is that season of life when you have children and the focus is on the next generation, and then grandchildren. It's a sobering question to ask: "Do I really want this man or woman I am going into a relationship with to be the parent of my children?"

Me Time prepares you for Us Time, and Us Time prepares you for Them Time. Make sure you complete what you can only do in your Me Time before you move into the Us Time. I wouldn't suggest that you need to be any specific age to be ready to move into the next stage, as this will differ vastly with different people. Again, please don't compare your age and stage to anyone else's. Live your own life at your own pace. Moving into the next stage because of pressure from someone else is crazy. The simple challenge with this is to do one season well before moving to the next. This takes wisdom and willingness to get a bit of a bigger picture view of your life, and not being consumed only with the moment you are in right now. To be a whole one is to be ready for *us*.

TIME TO REFLECT

To rephrase Andy Stanley's question: *Are you committed to becoming the whole one that the whole one you are looking for is looking for?*

I am well aware that you may have a deep longing for a partner. But I want to encourage you to not waste your single time pining away, wondering when you'll bump into Mr. or Mrs. Right. Your Me Time season is unique and special, and I want to encourage you to make the most of it. What you invest in your single days – your Me Time · you will richly reap in your Us Time, and the more there will be for you and your future spouse to withdraw when you do get married.

Become self-aware of areas where you can grow in wholeness. Consider sharing how you feel about these areas with a trusted friend, and ask them to help you to grow where you don't quite feel or act as a whole one. Make yourself vulnerable and accountable to them.

Do a serious evaluation if you are stuck in a "not-a-whole-one" relationship. If you are feeling manipulated or pressured by someone to do what you don't want to or to be who you are not, then I have some very kind and helpful pastoral advice for you: Run! Leave! (And do them a big favour by leaving a copy of DateTalk behind to help them grow into their own wholeness!)

Make a commitment today to grow in your personal wholeness. It's the best preparation for a relationship. Keep becoming the person that the person you are looking for is looking for.

GOD

The Bible is full of stories about Jesus meeting people whose lives were in a total mess relationally. Remember that woman caught in the act of adultery,[25] and the woman at the well, who had had five husbands?[26] These encounters are really helpful to reflect on if you wonder how God will relate to you when you bring your own relational mess and brokenness to him. Another woman has a man-eater reputation in her town, yet one day she is so tired of her mess that she boldly gatecrashes a party where Jesus is the honoured guest. She comes to him in faith, and he says to her: "Go in peace, your faith has made you well."[27] The meaning of the Greek word for peace is "wholeness." It has the sense of shattered pieces coming together as a whole. The Hebrew word for peace is "shalom" which literally means "nothing missing, nothing broken." I encourage you: whatever brokenness you have, or whatever mess from the past, bring it to God. Admit your mess, and ask his forgiveness for what you have done. Trust him and receive his peace and let him make you whole. This is the first step of becoming ready for a future fulfilled relationship.

The DateTalk Truth:

The best preparation you can make for a future relationship is a commitment to personal wholeness

Pause to think and talk it through:

- What one thing did you find most helpful or insightful in this chapter?

- Which of the "I am/I have" statements do you find most difficult for yourself, and why? (I have a life; I am loved; I am unique; I am a man/woman; I am valuable; I have left; I am ready for us.)

- What is one thing that you will apply to your own relationship journey from this chapter?

Chapter Four

UNDERSTANDING THE OPPOSITE SEX

I n the beginning He created them male and female.[28]

Men may not be from Mars or women from Venus,[29] but it often sure feels like it! We are different, and one of our greatest challenges in relationships and life is to understand those who are different to us. Understanding these differences is vital to having healthy relationships. A cynic once said that there are two times men and women don't understand each other: Before marriage and after marriage!

One of our deepest human longings is to feel known, and when you make the effort to understand the other, you will take huge strides towards building great relationships. What I'm encouraging you to do is commit yourself to be a learner, because to be a great lover you need to be a committed learner.

Now, I realise no one likes being put in a box, and I'm certainly not wanting to do that to you. But at the same time, there are reasons that stereotypes exist, and if there's any truth in them, it might help us men and women to understand each other better. So cut me some slack here perhaps, and see if any of these generalisations might apply to you (even if you'd prefer not to admit it!)

I once heard a joke about whether computers are male or female. A language instructor was explaining to her class that French nouns, unlike their English counterparts, are grammatically designated as masculine or feminine. Things like 'chalk' or 'pencil,' she described, would have a gender association although in English these words were neutral. Puzzled, one student raised his hand and asked, "What gender is a computer?" The teacher wasn't certain which it was, and so divided the class into two groups and asked them to decide if a computer should be masculine or feminine. One group comprised the girls in the class and the other, the guys. Both groups were asked to give four reasons for their recommendation. The group of girls concluded that computers should be referred to in the masculine gender because:

1. They are supposed to help you solve your problems, but half the time they ARE the problem!
2. They have a lot of data but are still clueless!
3. In order to get their attention, you have to turn them on!
4. As soon as you commit to one, you realise that, if you had waited a little longer, you could have had a better model!

The guys, on the other hand, decided that computers should definitely be referred to in the feminine gender because:

1. No one but their creator understands their internal logic!

2. The native language they use to communicate with other computers is incomprehensible to everyone else!

3. Even your smallest mistakes are stored in long-term memory for later retrieval!

4. As soon as you make a commitment to one, you find yourself spending half your salary on accessories for it!

One of our greatest needs in relationships is the need to be understood. I am convinced that if men understood women a little better, and women understood men a little better, it would go a long way to improving relationships. I once heard a great piece of advice: "Do not reject what you do not understand, for with understanding there may come acceptance."

One of our greatest needs in relationships is the need to be understood

Before we look at the differences though, it's also very important to understand two things we all have in common. If you don't pay attention to these two areas, you are sure to mess up any potential relationship.

The first deep need we share is the need for acceptance and belonging. "I am fully loved" and "I am fully known" is something every human deeply desires to be able to say. To be fully known · warts and all · and yet be fully loved and accepted, is one of the most satisfying human experiences. We all have a need-to-be-loved-tank inside, and any meaningful relationship must fulfil this need.

The second deep need all humans share is the need for significance and value. I need to be able to say that "I matter" or "I have significance". We all have a need to sense that our lives have meaning and value. I would go even further to suggest that all of us made in God's image have a deep need to feel that our lives matter not just now, but also in eternity. *Eat, drink and be merry*[30] just does not fill that void in anyone, whether male or female.

Any worthwhile relationship should meet these two needs. If a relationship you are in leaves you empty of feeling loved, or breaks down your sense of significance, my advice would be that you urgently initiate a serious conversation and express that these needs are not being satisfied.

Another similarity worth mentioning is that according to Gary Chapman in his bestselling book *The Five Love Languages,* we all have a love-tank. The big idea is that each of us "feels loved" in one of 5 ways, these being:

Receiving gifts

Acts of service

Words of affirmation

Quality time

Physical touch

He argues that it is important in any relationship to understand what specifically makes the other person feel loved - their primary love language - and then to make sure that we intentionally do that for them. The problem is that what fills my love tank may not be what fills yours. I may be a petrol car, and you a diesel, and as I have personally found out at great cost, a diesel car doesn't run well when you fill it up with petrol!

When we don't take the time to understand the other, our default is to give to them what *we* want or would like to receive *ourselves*. When this doesn't satisfy them, we think that they are ungrateful or unreasonable because they don't appreciate our efforts in love.

For example, early in our marriage, I used to think that doing chores around the house earned me some valuable points in our relationship. I'd come home after a long day at work and diligently get stuck into helping clean up the kitchen after a messy day with the kids. My wife appreciated it but my efforts never seemed to get the response that I expected. Then I discovered this idea of love languages and realised that Ali's primary love language is quality time. Acts of service were appreciated, but didn't really fill her love tank. What she really wanted when I got home was to first give her some focussed quality time catching up on our day, before getting busy doing stuff for her. For Ali, quality time fills her more than my acts of service. It doesn't mean that I don't need to do my chores, but it does mean that I don't expect her to feel deeply loved just because I washed the dishes! For Ali, quality time with focused attention says *I love you* much louder than washing the dishes does. So what did I do? Well, of course, I went and bought a dishwasher!

Now let's get back to those differences. The Manual says that both the male and the female variety of the human species consists of three main elements: body, soul, and spirit, which can be explained as follows: The body is our flesh; that part which hurts when you pinch it. It's the part of us that is connected to and interacts with this material world. The soul is our subconscious self, including our mind, emotions (our feelings) and will. The spirit is the part of us that connects with the spiritual and that which is beyond this material and self-world. It's the God-conscious, God-seeking, God-relating part. The spirit is the part which draws us to what we call worship.

Let's try to understand the similarities, and the differences in each of these, starting with the body.

BODY

Have you noticed that the bodies of the opposite sex are a little different? Of course they are. Men are generally stronger, and women are just naturally prettier and have a more attractive shape. Adam got a roughened up chiselled look, and Eve got some curves. The male and female plumbing is different. Penises and vaginas. And breasts. God created us as sexual creatures. The Manual says that these two different bodies would be united physically, with

Adam exclaiming when he first set eyes on Eve that she would be *"Bone of my bone, flesh of my flesh!"*

The physical form and function of the male and female body and how they are designed to fit and function together seem to me to be Divine design at its very best, and a compelling signpost pointing to a Divine Creator.

Our sexuality does some crazy things to our bodies. We get turned on. Sexually aroused. Both the male and the female body is perfectly designed for sexual pleasure and procreation, but to avoid a lot of destructive fire when these sparks start flying you have to understand something about how men and women respond and are turned on differently. Men are like gas stoves, which when you turn them on are virtually instantly ready for cooking. Women are more like electric stoves, which take a lot longer to heat up, and you really have to monitor them to see when they are ready for cooking. Once they are hot, they take a while to cool down! Men, on the other hand, go cold very quickly once it's over, just like a gas stove.

Let me give you some more help with this dilemma.

Men are predominantly turned on by sight and suggestion. For women, it's much more by words, touch and atmosphere. That's why advertisers always use skimpily clad girls to sell things to guys. Everything from cars to magazines to lawn mowers is offered to men by a beautiful hardly-dressed woman to get their attention and their cash. This is, of course, a terrible objectification of women, but advertisers know how it works and they exploit this to the max. On the other hand, have you noticed what they use to sell things to women? Not a hot guy in a Speedo. No, they use romance. They use a guy who is dressed to the T, rose in hand with romantic music playing in the background while the candlelight illuminates the product being offered to the ladies.

Different things get our attention, and it's vital to understand this in your relationship journey. For example, take the guy who needs help with his homework and asks a girl he is friends with to help him. He has no other intentions but to get help with his maths problem. Not thinking, he chooses a quiet, tasteful coffee shop as the location. The lights are low, soft music plays in the background, and there are candles on the table. While he has said that he wants help with his maths, the setting he has chosen is sending a completely different message to the girl. The atmosphere may not mean much to him, but to her, it's oozing with romance and seductively saying *I'm interested in you. I want you.* His total cluelessness has set them up for some potentially awkward misunderstanding. If you don't want to send that message, then don't allow your actions to speak louder than your words, and make sure that your words make the message you do want to send very clear. And, if you don't want to do any explaining, then just take her to McDonald's to solve that maths problem instead!

Here's how it works with the girls. She wants some help with her science problem and asks her guy friend to meet up at McDonald's for a milkshake to help her solve her problem. She has no feelings for him and just wants his help with her science. Seems simple enough, until she arrives with the tiniest of outfits showing loads of leg, cleavage and midriff. It's a formula for turning on any man, and while she may just want to talk science over a milkshake in McDonald's, the man is hearing a completely different message from her. Now she has more than a science problem!

The Manual warns us to not "defraud" one another. To defraud means to promise something that you are not willing or able to deliver on. Often this is done in ignorance because we simply do not understand how our actions are interpreted by the other person. If it's done intentionally, then this is called flirting, or another word for it may be *lying* because you are sending a message that you have no intention to fulfil.

We will still do a lot of talking about sex in chapter six, but for now, there's one more thing you must know about the body, and your body. Culture has its ever changing way of determining who and what is attractive and sexy and what is not. But here's a truth I stated earlier in the book: *Everybody is sexy to somebody*. You are attractive to the right person for you. Be confident in your body. Look after yourself, and present yourself well, but please, please don't become a slave to the image of this world in order to attract someone. Sure, stay tuned to fashion, but don't become a slave to it. The most attractive you that you can be is you. Remember, you are unique, and your body is sexy to somebody!

Now let's talk about the soul.

SOUL

Remember, this is your subconscious self, including your mind, emotions and will. This is where things get very interesting, and differences abound. There are definitely *he-motions* and *she-motions*, and they are very different. This is also where I will totally over-generalise, so please remember that I am doing this simply to make you aware of the importance of understanding that the other whom you are interested in is different to you, and to provoke you to become a learner so that you can be a better lover.

There is a theory about the differences in the soul of men and women. Let me explain:

When a baby is born and you want to know whether it's a boy or girl, you can't hear it in the way the baby looks or cries. The only difference is the genitalia.

A few days after birth though, something very strange happens, but only in the male baby.

A chemical called testosterone starts flowing through the male body, and it begins to attack the fibres that connect the two sides of the male brain. What it does, is it destroys some of the connecting fibres between the left and right side of the brain. Remember, this happens only in the innocent male baby!

The result of this testosterone attack is that the right and left sides of the male brain are not so well connected, and because of this, a man tends to be able to use only one side of the brain at a time when he thinks. (Some women would say that's not very often.) Also, the testosterone shrinks the right side of the brain, which is the side which tends to process more feelings, while the left side processes more logically. As a result, men are generally governed more by the left side of their brain. Ali has an easy way of helping me remember which side of the brain a man uses more, right or left. She says: "The man is not right!"

Now I want to assure you that this is true medical fact · or at least it is an explanation for the reality that men tend to be more "compartmental" and women more "global" in their processing of life. Because we men are not completely connected upstairs, we have an enviable ability to easily separate things and situations into different compartments. I can switch off to one area while I fully focus on another. A woman though does not have the privilege of a disconnected brain. She is still fully connected using both parts of her brain, so everything affects everything. All that is going on in her world flows together like streams into one big river. If one thing is bothering her, everything is wrong and life's a mess. That's why words like "always" and "never" are so much more part of a woman's vocabulary than a typical man's. By the way, here's a tip that I have learnt from much personal painful experience. When someone uses those words, you have to hear them as "feeling words" and not "fact words." A wise man will hear and respond to what she is feeling, and not argue that *never* is not factually correct because he actually did do it once ... a long time ago. Hear the feelings, not the "facts".

Also, because of this the female species comes with that incredible (and sometimes very confusing to men) characteristic called intuition. This is the result of the rational and emotional sides working together. She's more sensitive, and she feels things the man has absolutely no clue about. While my two semi-disconnected brain parts are slowly communicating and figuring something out, Ali has already "sensed" it a long time ago!

The right side of the brain · the one a little shrunken in the man · is more focused on feelings and emotions, helping with things like being more relational, nurturing, and remembering names. Have you ever noticed at what point a woman starts to enjoy or show interest when they are watching a sports game? It's as soon as she knows one of the player's names. David. Johnny. The guys love the conquest. Go England! Then a guy may shout something like "Come on David!" and the girl will say, "Which one is David?" Once she knows a name, it's game on. Go, David! Go, Johnny!

The left side of the brain · the one still mostly intact in the man · is more conqueror and challenge oriented. Every man needs a battle to fight. He wants to conquer. Like when you are on a road trip, the guy will typically be focussed on the destination and how fast he can get there (and is that faster than his mate did it?), while the girl typically wants to enjoy the journey and hanging out.

We also shop differently... but let's not even go there now!

Men and women also communicate differently. Men use headlines, while women want the details and the fine print. A man's vocabulary contains some favourite words · yes they are real words · like uh, ah, yip, ok. These are condensed words because each little word carries a whole lot of deep thought and emotion that the man is communicating. Unfortunately, even with their connected brain, women are not so good at interpreting the details and depth of these words!

We also handle crisis and solve problems differently. When a man has a problem, he retreats to his cave, because he feels the need to work it out by himself. He typically wants to find the solution on his own before he shares the problem. He wants to be the conqueror of the problem. If you try to get him to talk before he is ready, you will just cause him to retreat even further into his cave.

A woman on the other hand typically needs to share her problem and lay it out before all. But, she does not want you to give her a solution! NO NO NO. What she wants is for you to listen and to understand. She does not want a solution, just empathy. The man will tend to see her need as a great opportunity to be her knight in shining armour and will want to ride in and conquer her problem by offering a solution and fix it and rescue her.

So you can see the obvious clash: the man does not want to share his problem until he has a solution, and the woman gets her solution by sharing her problem. Simple isn't it!

The lesson to men here may just be that the way a man uses his ears is a very, very attractive thing for a woman, and if you learn to use them well your success in a relationship could really improve!

SPIRIT

So we've looked at the body and the soul, and now let's finally look at the spirit. Remember, this is the God-conscious, God-seeking, God-relating part of you. It's that part of our being that draws us to what we call worship. I propose to you that this is the most significant thing that distinguishes us as human, rather than merely evolved animals. You see, wherever you find any form of humanity, you find an expression of worship, but this is not the case with any animals. They have bodies and souls - emotions, a will, a mind - but they have no spirit because there is no evidence or expression anywhere in the animal kingdom of worship. Ok, maybe a praying mantis, but that's about it!

According to the Manual, man and woman are both created in God's image for relationship with him[31]. This makes us exactly the same in our spirits; able to know God and relate to him personally and intimately as individuals. St Augustine said it this way: *"You have made us for yourself O God, and our hearts are restless until they find their rest in you."*

Now, I'm sure you have heard that when you are pursuing a relationship, it is important to find your soulmate and that you should be careful to consider whether you are compatible intellectually, emotionally, economically, some even suggest sexually (more of that in chapter six). But here's a question: How important is it to be spiritually compatible with a future life mate? If you are a believer in Jesus Christ, this would mean someone who shares your most important passion, your real relationship with God. I personally believe, from my convictions as well as from observing and counselling many people, that this is indeed a most important area in which to find compatibility and agreement. Without it, you will lose out on sharing one huge and very meaningful part of your life with someone you are committing to completely.

In summary, I would propose to anyone planning to have an exclusively committed relationship or planning to get married that it is very important to find common ground and agreement in spiritual matters.

As we close this chapter on understanding the opposite sex, I want to ask you to make a commitment to keep being a learner in relationships. To become a better lover, you must keep growing as a learner. Go back over this chapter and let some of the thoughts prompt you to recognise some specific areas in which you need to grow in understanding. One way to grow as a learner is to grow as a listener. Be interested. Be curious. Don't just stay locked up looking at things from your own point of view and your own point of need. To be listened to and to be loved are almost indistinguishable; that's why good listeners make good lovers.

The DateTalk Truth:

To be a better lover, you must become a better learner

Pause to think and talk it through:

- What one thing did you find most helpful or insightful in this chapter?

- Which of the stereotypical male/female generalisations seemed to describe you? Which didn't? Did any of them surprise you?

- What one thing do you find most difficult to understand about the opposite sex? How has something from this chapter helped you think differently about this specific issue?

- What is one thing that you will apply to your own relationship journey from this chapter?

Chapter Five

LESSONS FROM LOVERS' LANE

We are made for relationship. We have a desire to be joined together. But how can we do it well? How can we make sure we don't mess ourselves and others up along the way?

The next part of our journey is a look at how and why dating so often goes wrong. In this chapter, we will focus on some crucial things to avoid if we want to do relationships well. Then in chapter seven, we will look at *a better way*.

There are always two ways to do something:

The right way and the wrong way.

The easy way and the difficult way.

The wise way and the foolish way.

The way that leads to life, and a way that leads to death.

The high way or the low way.

The holy way or the Hollywood way.

The love way or the lust way.

The God's will way or the my will way.

For the sake of terminology in DateTalk, I will refer to the right way as The HighWay, and the wrong way as Lovers' Lane. The HighWay is the way that we start out on. We're trying to do everything the right way, holding to our core values, taking things at the right tempo · even waiting patiently for the right moment. We'll talk about The HighWay later · but for now, I want to focus on Lovers' Lane, which represents all the shortcuts, distractions and temptations that will try to lure us off The HighWay, onto a route that seems like a good idea at the time, but before long, the place that Lovers' Lane leads you to might not seem so good after all. The reason we will talk about this negative way first is to make sure that you know what you don't want, so that you may be more keen to learn how you can do it better.

So let's look at what typically happens on this "two people getting together" journey. As always, it begins right inside you and works its way out into actions and consequences, either good or bad. Please remember that we are looking for principles here and not a formula.

Here's what the typical dating pattern looks like:

- Confusion Lane
- Compromise Corner
- The Chase
- Home Alone

- Passion Rules
- The Crash

Let's look at each of these and see what lessons you can learn to avoid messing up this wonderfully exciting but often confusing relationship journey.

CONFUSION LANE

It's a powerful thing when you can get your thinking right about something before you face it, but relationship trouble usually starts with confusion, when you have not made up your mind what you want and don't want, and what is right and what is not. Such as whether it's right to take her to that late-night romantic movie, or whether it's right to wear that particularly low-cut dress that you think might work its magic on him. Or the place and purpose of sex in a relationship. The problem with living in a state of confusion or uncertainty is that you don't have any clarity to guide you in your choices and decision making. If you don't know the right way, then any way will do. When you are not clear about your values, hopes, dreams, convictions, etc. then you are vulnerable to be led by your passions in any direction they will take you.

The problem is that most of us never got much good advice about how to do relationships well. Hollywood, TV soaps, gossip magazines and music videos are among the many powerful relationship teachers of our day, but at best what you learn from them leads to confusion and lust, not clarity and love. You have to decide to find a trusted teacher to help you do relationships right. Again, I suggest that the Maker is best positioned to teach you, and if you are willing to listen and learn, his Manual has much helpful truth and advice to guide you out of confusion and into clarity. It's always your choice whether to live out the lessons or to reject them. Unfortunately, though, we *don't* get to choose the consequences of our choices. Confusion is the soil in which compromise grows.

Confusion is the soil in which compromise grows

COMPROMISE CORNER

The compromise we are talking about here is where you sacrifice your very best to get something you know is not as good. Why would anyone do that? Well, perhaps the cost of time, or effort, or patience to get the very best seems too high. Or perhaps we start to doubt that the very best will ever happen, and start to look at our second or third best ideas. As you journey through life on The HighWay with your values, hopes, dreams, expectations and a desire to do things the right way, you will inevitably encounter some troubles. There will be some delays, disappointments, discouragements, and each of these will tempt you to leave The HighWay. Desperation will start to whisper that it is time to take the next exit and try an alternative way. You will persevere for a while, but more trouble and delay will cause the voice of desperation to get louder and louder, urging you to turn off now!

A guy who had made some terrible decisions with some destructive consequences once said to me, "Wolfi, I had messed up, and if I was honest it was because I was desperate." You may do this because you fear that you are going to be single for the rest of your life. Or when your friends seem to all be pairing up, and there just don't seem to be any suitable guys or girls where you hang around. You may start to think: *I'm the only single person left! I'm going to be single for the rest of my life! I'll never find someone! No one likes me! There must be something wrong with me!* This makes you feel that you are past your sell-by date, and you know what shopkeepers do when an item gets to its sell-by date, don't you? They lower the price and try to sell it at a discount, often far below its value, just to get it off the shelf. Don't do that to yourself. Stay on The HighWay. That's the only place you want to find your helper.

When you are confused and desperate, you are very likely to turn off The HighWay and take a trip down Lovers' Lane. You start with the Maker's promise, but when the going gets a little tough, you are tempted to try to add something to the promise in an attempt to find a quicker and easier way to your happiness. You lower your standards, expectations, principles, values, and sadly in your attempt to make it better, you generally end up spoiling the promise. When you give up on your dreams, you often end up settling for a nightmare.

Please note that I am talking here about compromising your real core values, rather than compromising your idealistic wish list of what you want in a partner. Love will mess with your wish list in a big, beautiful way as opposites attract and all that, but true love will not require you to compromise what is core and most important to you.

By the way, whenever you do decide to go around Compromise Corner, there will always be a bunch of people telling you it's the right thing to do. Be warned though: When you follow the crowd, you're also likely to lose yourself in it.

THE CHASE

Once confusion has led you to compromise, compromise will get you chasing. This part of Lovers' Lane is when you begin to obsess about your need to have a relationship and find that right person. It becomes your main and all consuming thing. Please don't misunderstand me: Of course you want to meet new people. One of the joys of being single is the expectation of meeting that someone special. It's perfectly normal to want to find Mr. or Mrs. Right. It's good to position yourself to meet new people, and you may even register on a dating site. Or three. That's all ok, as long as you are doing this as a "whole one" who has a life. (Remember this from chapter three?)

The Chase is different to the normal desire for a relationship because it's motivated by the myth that you need to have a boy/girlfriend to be fulfilled and accepted. Here you start to believe that you must have someone in order to be someone. It assumes that you do not have a life if you do not have a boy/girlfriend. When your relational status is becoming the primary measure of your self-worth, then you know that you have turned off The HighWay and onto the slippery slope of The Chase.

Typically, The Chase is characterised by shallow talk and flirting. You start hiding the real you, pretending to be someone different to who you are, because you start believing that the real you isn't good relationship material. You basically end up playing the hypocrite, pretending to be somebody you're not.

Remember 10-year-old Mike who was asked: *What do people do on the first date?* He answered: "Usually they tell one another lies. That normally gets them interested enough to go on a second date!"

Why do we start telling lies or even start living as great pretenders? Because we're afraid of rejection. We're afraid that the other person won't like me if they know who I really am, warts and all. Of course, the problem is that the other person will at some stage discover the real you if the relationship goes anywhere, and that's going to be awkward for both of you. The Chase is simply not a good way to find a future partner who is eventually going to discover everything about you.

If you do continue The Chase and happen to catch someone in your pursuit, your next stop on Lovers' Lane is probably going to be what I will call Home Alone.

HOME ALONE

This part of Lovers' Lane is often characterised by isolation, and "I" becomes the most important factor. Here's how it tends to happen: Because of The Chase mentality of insecurity and desperation, when people on The Chase meet and start dating, they usually quite quickly withdraw from others and are very protective or possessive about their new relationship. You start to keep those previously close to you at arm's length. You have less and less time for friends and family, and you can't understand why some of them are worried about you. You definitely don't want to have any meaningful conversations with anyone close to you about what is going on in your new relationship. This is when love really gets blind, and you can't see what is happening because when two desperate people have gotten together, they want to do everything they can to keep what they have got and prevent anyone else from interfering or giving advice.

It's like in those wildlife documentaries where you see a leopard stalk its prey, catch it, and drag the carcass high into a tree in an attempt to keep others from sharing its lunch. Because of the underlying fear of being alone, you isolate yourself and close your ears and eyes and hope this is right because you can't risk losing what you have.

It usually doesn't take much for Home Alone to lead to a place on Lovers' Lane where Passion Rules.

PASSION RULES

This is where sexual passion takes over the driving seat on your relationship journey. It usually doesn't take much for isolation and emotional involvement to quickly lead to physical involvement. Kissing, snogging, French kissing. Hands on body parts which you don't have yourself. Clothes off. Mutual masturbation. Sex. Orgasms. It's nice, it's passionate, it's arousing, and it starts taking over. At this stage the isolated pair experience what the authors of *The Ten Commandments of Dating*[32] call "BRP" - The "Brain Relocation Phenomenon," in which you start reasoning with your genitals instead of your brain. The onset of this phenomenon usually takes about ten to twenty minutes for a woman and one or two minutes for a guy. Before BRP kicks in, you had values and good intentions and wanted to do things a certain way. Now all that is gone out the window as you get swept away by your passions. One problem is that guys and girls are SO different in this department. He is typically ready to connect physically long before he is ready to commit emotionally. A girl will often give herself physically in the expectation that the guy will commit emotionally, but she doesn't know what a disconnected brain he's got and that the right side where emotion is activated is a little shrunken and depleted. Just because you give him your body does not mean that he will give you his soul.

Some girls will use their sexual allure to trap a guy. You know what he wants and you give it to him, but really you are just using him to feed your own insecurity and ego.

During Passion Rules those three little words *I love you* are often whispered in a low trying-to-be-sexy voice. But as Passion Rules, these should be more accurately interpreted as "I want you", or even more accurately: "I like it." This is where the Lovers' Lane journey gets really dangerous. You say "I like it" but you are not even sure that you like him, or her. Even if you start to discover things about your date which you don't really like, often the physical bond keeps you together. Instead of getting to know each other's soul, you are enjoying each other's bodies. One reality that every person involved in a relationship has to discover at some point is that sex, physical involvement and attraction are not enough to make a relationship or a marriage work. Ask any couple that has been married for a number of years if it's their sex life that keeps them together, and the answer will be no. Of course, it's vitally important, and great when it is working well, but it takes much, much more than sex to keep two people together.

Sex can't "make love." It can only express it. Sex is either an expression of love or an expression of lust. Love gives, and lust takes. Most of what we see on the big screen is not making love, but making lust. Just because a man has sex with a prostitute does not mean he loves her. No, he just lusts her.

Sex can't "make love." It can only express it.

It is helpful here to understand that in the Greek language in which most of the New Testament of the Manual was written, there are at least three different words to express three different kinds of love. These are eros, phileo, and agape: Eros expresses the romantic, erotic, sensual, sexual passion; the physical aspect of love. Phileo expresses friendship, companionship, communication, sharing, caring, talking, listening aspects of love. Agape is the God kind of love. It is vast in its meaning, but for our purposes here understand it as the expression of unconditional and selfless love. It says things like "what's mine is yours" and "until death parts us."

Imagine that your relationship is a play and that you and your significant other are on a stage. Phileo, Agape and Eros make up the rest of the cast and are waiting in the wings for their big moment to join you on the stage. You are also the director and must give the cues for when each of them comes onto the stage to join the play. The correct order would be to let Phileo love come on first. At this point you need to watch Eros carefully because Eros is a very impatient member of the cast, always waiting behind the curtain wanting desperately to rush onto the stage and join the play. But that would seriously complicate and possibly even ruin the play, so Eros must wait offstage until its cue, which is only once Agape says the two magic words, "I do." This is the best and proper time for Eros to rush onto the stage and complete the play!

Eros's cue is not the three words "I love you", nor is it the two words "I will". Only "I do" at the altar will do. Let me say it in another way to all you ladies: Don't lay down your body with him until he has lain down his life for you, with two magic words "I do." The point is simply this: Do not allow physical intimacy to take the centre stage of your relationship until you are sure Phileo and Agape are playing the major parts. If you get this order wrong, you will end up liking and knowing your significant other's body, but you certainly won't know their soul and their spirit, and that is simply never going to be good enough for a meaningful relationship.

What did the original girl band the Spice Girls really want when they sang, "I tell you what I want, what I really, really want"? All the sensualised media backup to the song communicates that it was all about sex. But what do we really, really want? The truth is that what any girl or guy · including you · really, really wants is real intimacy. We long for intimacy, and true intimacy is about being fully known. You see, you will only ever feel fully loved when you feel that you are fully known, soul to soul, not just body to body. Sex can never say I love you like you truly need to hear it. I will say that again a few more times in this book because you really, really need to hear and believe it.

You will only ever feel fully loved when you feel that you are fully known.

If you let Eros get in ahead of Phileo and Agape, it is virtually guaranteed that you will struggle to develop true intimacy, because you will confuse physical intimacy with true intimacy, and sex can never give you true intimacy and say *I love you* like you need to hear it deep on the inside of you. When Passion Rules it may be nice on the night and it will seem to be scratching the itch for intimacy, but it will never take the itch away. In fact, it is more likely to hinder true intimacy than to help it.

Passion Rules often leads to saying that you have "fallen in love". The problem is that falling in love on Lovers' Lane often ends up in a dead end, which we will call The Crash.

THE CRASH

One morning our then 8-year-old daughter came into our bedroom at 6 am and said: "I had such a nice dream, but now it's over..." Sadly, falling in love on Lovers' Lane is often a setup for falling out of love, leaving at least one broken heart behind. This pairing up, isolation, and getting physical is a major risk. What if he isn't Mr. Right? Face it, you're not bound to bump into Mr. Right while you're snogging Mr. Wrong down some dark alley, are you? There are three problems with this typical Lovers' Lane dating pattern.

First, the assumption that you need to have a boy/girlfriend to be somebody makes you a very dependent and desperate person. You are never fully at ease with yourself because you are always positioning yourself like a salesperson at a party looking for any opportunity to sell something. That's just not very attractive.

Second, you miss out on the joy of genuine friendships. Lovers' Lane leaves little room for no-strings-attached friendships with the opposite sex in order to get to know people without the pressure of "who should I be going out with".

Third, if this pattern repeats itself in your life it can have some serious negative short and long-term results. Our sexual and emotional desires were not designed to be ignited and snuffed out, started and then stopped with different people. Giving your body to someone here, then someone else there will only result in confusion in your soul because you simply were not designed to join and separate, join and separate. When you let that happen you sow seeds of rejection, separation, and shallowness into your future.

The Lovers' Lane dating pattern can be summed up by the old little English nursery rhyme:

Georgie Porgie pudding and pie, kissed the girls and made them cry.

When the boys came out to play, Georgie Porgie ran away...

This is pretty much the typical result of the Lovers' Lane attempt at dating, leaving the girls crying and the boys running away. The boys are running scared and unsure of themselves, and the girls are emotionally wrecked. If you are one of those who is crying or running away, I want to say to you: There is a better way!

Dating doesn't have to be that way and it doesn't have to end that way. There is an alternative, and in chapter eight called "The HighWay" I'll show you what that better way looks like. But first, we need to do some straight talking about sex.

The DateTalk Truth:

There is a better way!

Pause to think and talk about it:

What one thing did you find most helpful or insightful in this chapter?

Evaluate your own journey down Lovers' Lane with the following questions:

- Are you clear about what you want and value in relationships, or are you wandering down Confusion Lane?

- Have you gone around Compromise Corner because you have become desperate or discouraged by delay?

- Have you become obsessed with The Chase, believing the lie that you have to have someone to be someone?

- Have you got stuck Home Alone with someone, and stopped investing in genuine friendships?

- Has Passion Rules taken over in your relationship?

- Have you experienced hurt and disappointment in relationships, causing you to withdraw and lose hope for your future?

What is one thing that you will apply to your own relationship journey from this chapter?

Chapter Six

SEXTALK

There is one thing that accompanies us all along this relationship journey, and that is our sexual desire. It's normal to have a sex drive. But where does it best fit along the relationship journey? What do I do with these feelings? Does the Manual have anything helpful to say about this? These are all good questions and I want to explore these with you in this chapter. It's going to be straight talk, so if you are not ready for that, you'd better put this book down now!

Everyone has their own sex story.

Some have never had sex.

Some have done it once or a few times.

Some are doing it regularly in a marriage relationship.

Some are married and not doing it so regularly.

Some are not married and doing it regularly.

Some feel OK being sexually active because they are in a committed relationship, and others don't feel OK about that but can't seem to stop it.

Some don't actually do it but fantasise about it and quite a few are virtually doing it through pornography and sexually explicit stuff they are reading.

Most of the above have been in heterosexual relationships, but some are in same sex situations.

The reality is that each of us has our own sexual history, and we each live with its positive or negative consequences today in our bodies, our minds, and our emotions. What we have to figure out is how we make our passions serve us well in our relationships, rather than us being slaves to them.

In the wisdom book of The Song of Solomon, the Manual paints this picture of a man and woman in an intense moment of passion: (Don't ever say the Bible is boring!)

His left hand is under my head, and his right hand embraces me.[33]

They are all over each other, ready to let Passion Rule, but then she cries out:

I charge you, O daughters of Jerusalem, by the gazelles or by the does of the field, do not stir up nor awaken love until it pleases.

For the point I'm making here, translate this as *I'm being swept off my feet, but someone please help me do this right, and at the right time!* Another Wisdom book in the Manual assures us that *"God makes everything beautiful in itself and in its time"*[34] Solomon's girl is encouraging all who will listen that there is a right time for passion, but the time is not always right.

Speaking of timing, you may have wondered why God your Maker didn't just add a switch somewhere so that sexual passions could simply be activated only at the right time. But you have to understand that our sexuality is something we desperately need throughout our relationship journey, and I'll tell you why. Firstly, sexual attraction is a good thing because it's part of the initial chemistry that attracts people to one another and reminds you that you were created for relationship. Secondly, when things go wrong on the relationship journey and we get hurt and disappointed, we tend to withdraw into a castle and pull up the drawbridge to try to protect ourselves from getting hurt again. This is not how we were created to live though, and it is often our sexual attraction that draws us back out to at least peep over the walls that we have built and reminds us that it is not good to be alone and to try again.

Of course, as this happens you need wisdom and truth to help you navigate the rapids of your passions so that they take you to where you really want to be, rather than somewhere that you never set out to go in the first place. More of that later. For now, just say again: *I need help!*

I know that many people think that all you need is the right "How far can I go?" rules, but these are rarely helpful. If you are going to change your understanding and attitude towards sex and sexuality, you will need revelation, not rules. Revelation is when you get to grips (excuse the pun) with a deep understanding of the truth about something, knowing that "this really is the best way!!" I could give you a bunch of rules, like: *"Don't take any clothes off and don't touch anything you haven't got yourself."* Or, *"Treat her like your sister, and him like your brother."* But rules will always be broken. They may stop some actions for a while, but rules won't deal with your inner struggle. Yes, we do need boundaries, but more than that we need the power of purpose.

When you have a strong purpose for sticking to your core beliefs, that purpose can give you strength to stick to them; to say "no" or "not yet" to the things that aren't ok for now, and "yes" to the good, healthy things that are best for this time. You need to decide what is most important to you: maturing your relationship, or following your sexual passions.

You need more than rules. You need revelation to help you deal with this subject of sex and to experience it as a huge blessing in your own relationship journey.

To do this we will look at three crucial areas:

1. Myths about sex
2. The manual on sex
3. The mystery of sex

MYTHS ABOUT SEX

First, you need to decide what your sources about sex are so you can think clearly about these things. You need to decide whether you believe the myths or the Manual. The fact is, we are bombarded with (false) information about sex from every side and in huge doses. Let's consider some of the myths about sex, as promoted by many movies, TV shows, books, glossy magazines, music videos, pop-up ads, other advertising, and all porn. You may or may not actually believe these myths, but please do consider whether any of these influenced your thinking about sex.

The Make Love Myth

This myth says that you can make love through sex. But you can't. At best, sex can only express love, not make love. If there is no love, sex will never make love happen. If he can't love you without sex, he will not love you with sex. To love is not the same as to lie down with someone. Think about it: Why do so many people, as they lie there in the arms of someone they have just had sex with, still ask, "Do you love me?" The reason is that sex can never say "I love you" like you need to hear it. Love is not made in a momentary high, but in what happens before, and what happens after. Sex is nothing more than lust (gratifying self at the expense of another) if one of the parties involved reserves the right to reject the other the following day. Unconditional commitment is what really makes love, not sex. This "make love" myth must be busted if you are going to experience real love because sex will never be enough.

The Safe Sex Myth

This myth assumes that sex is just something the body takes part in. It assumes that you are just body, and forgets the soul and the spirit. The focus of this myth is about protecting the body from the possible effects of sex, like pregnancy and STDs · Sexually Transmitted Diseases. (Yes, these are real, and very serious in many cases, and not so sexy either.)

There has never been a condom invented that protects the mind and heart. Sex is never just a physical activity.

Just imagine someone finding out that their significant other is sleeping with someone else. It's not like they are just having lunch or going for a run together, is it? There is definitely much more to sex than the physical.

Did you ever watch the movie Indecent Proposal? (Not recommended by the way). In it, a married couple is in desperate financial need, and a wealthy businessman makes them a proposal that he will give them a million dollars for one night of sex with the wife. This could solve all their problems, and as the couple argue and discuss the offer she tries to reason by saying that "I'm only giving him my body, not my soul." But it doesn't work, does it? Point made. God alone created safe sex, and he called it marriage between a man and a woman. It's safe for the individuals, it's safe for the couple, and it's a safe place for the arrival of a baby (or babies!)

The Try Before You Buy Myth

This myth says that it is important to explore whether you are sexually compatible with someone as part of committing to a serious relationship, especially marriage. It assumes that you can actually discover sexual compatibility in the same way as you can discover whether you are intellectually or socially compatible. So let me give you the real facts about sexual compatibility: You are sexually compatible, and you are also not sexually compatible. I'll explain this as clearly as I can. Firstly, the Maker designed the male and female body to fit together in sexual union in an amazing way. Arousing. Penis. Vagina. Clitoris. If a male and a female get together with sexual passion, they fit. Beautifully. It's been designed to work, and on the few occasions when there are complications, these can usually be solved medically or through mutual understanding or counselling. You probably will not discover these through a one night stand or a few drunken moments of passion.

On the other hand, we have already learnt that males and females get turned on differently, and it takes quite a lot of understanding to tune in to one another's needs and pleasures. Assessing a potential relationship by one or a few sexual encounters is simply a very poor measure. Also remember that as you are "trying" someone out, you are also being tried out, and you are both using each other. That kind of performance measuring is never a good formula for any healthy relationship. You definitely need to bust this myth, because there are a lot more important compatibility issues to consider in your journey to a healthy and happy relationship.

The Sex Gives Intimacy Myth

This myth claims that adding a sexual expression to your dating relationship will deepen the intimacy between you.

That's definitely true in marriage, but definitely not true in dating. In fact, sex in a dating relationship most often gets in the way of developing true intimacy in a dating relationship, rather than deepening it. You have to bust this myth if you want to make sure that you find the real intimacy that you need for laying a solid foundation in your relationship.

The Everybody is Doing It Myth

This myth proclaims that virginity is totally uncool and that there must be something seriously wrong or weird about you if you are not having sex at every opportunity, or at least in a committed relationship. It assumes that there is no need or point or value or reason to wait for "I do" before being sexually active. It's a message repeated over and over again in every love story of our culture, where sex is the next step after meeting someone, and that it's always wonderful. The reality is that there are many, many people who are realising that this myth is misleading and an empty promise. Everybody isn't doing it, and for many that are, sex is not doing it for them. They realise that sex can't deliver what it was never intended for. Many are saying, like Solomon's woman, "Do not stir up or awaken love until it pleases," and are believing the wisdom that "God makes everything good in its time."

I have the privilege of conducting many weddings and leading couples through marriage preparation. I always find that past sexual activity and the loss of virginity are huge issues for couples to work through. Many people have not bought into this myth, and are keeping their virginity for their wedding day. Many more have had sex in the past, but have come to see the value of their virginity, and have stopped having sex, to commit themselves to wholeness in this area. The myth busting fact is that many people are realising that sex before marriage short-circuits and jeopardises the relationship journey, and are committing themselves to what I call "temporary celibacy." (No more sex until my wedding day).

Don't settle for being an everybody in the crowd. Be a somebody, and keep yourself for the someone special. It will be worth it.

Those are some of the myths about sex, now let's see what we can learn from the Manual.

THE MANUAL ABOUT SEX

Most people think that all the Manual has to say about sex is *don't do it until you are married*, but that is a very limited understanding. Such a superficial treatment of this important subject will never be enough to guide you through your own passions and all the pressures you will face to do things differently. So let's look at what the Manual does instruct about sex, and what it warns about sex, and see what we can learn:

Here are a few things that the Manual says about sex:

- *Be fruitful & multiply*[35]
- *They were both naked and unashamed*[36]

- *Adam knew Eve and she conceived and bore a son*[37]
- *The marriage bed is undefiled*[38]

Right from the start the Manual tells us that God created sex because the only way Adam and Eve would be able to fulfil this purpose to be fruitful and multiply was through sexual intercourse. Sex was God's idea, and he thought - and still thinks - that it is a very good idea.

The Manual also says that *"Therefore a man will leave... and be joined to his wife..."*.[39] Wife, not girlfriend. The fruit from their sexual relationship is intended to be born into a secure covenant relationship between the man and his wife. God made us sexual beings, and the Manual also clearly prescribes the place and purpose of sex: In marriage and for procreation - having babies. It goes on to describe that "Adam knew Eve and she conceived and bore a son."[40] The word used here for *know* is the Hebrew *yada*, and it means much more than just having sexual intercourse. It means true knowing and intimacy. A sharing of the soul, not just the body. In the Bible, there's a big difference between "knowing" someone sexually, and "lying with someone" sexually. "Knowing" someone sexually is about love, and merely "lying" with someone sexually is about lust. True sex isn't just about "lying" with someone, but about truly "knowing" them. David "lay" with Bathsheba[41] but he did not "know" her. You can "lie" with someone, but never "know" them, and that is a very empty place. Many people have had sexual partners, but have never "known" anyone.

I heard a story about Marilyn Monroe, the famous sex symbol of the 1950s, who was once asked if she had ever really felt loved. Her answer is very revealing: "I've had many relationships, but I only felt loved once by a foster mother when I was young. As she touched me, I felt like I was loved." Wow, talk about sex not being enough.

In the New Testament part of the Manual, we read that *"Marriage should be honored by all, and the marriage bed kept pure."*[42] That's sex in the right place for the right purpose, and I think that when God said, "It is very good" at the end of creation, he was referring to this complete intimacy between the man and his wife being naked and unashamed.

In the Proverbs section of the Manual the wise man observes this beautiful thing:

> *Let your wife be a fountain of blessing for you. Rejoice in the wife of your youth. She is a loving deer, a graceful doe. Let her breasts satisfy you at all times. May you always be captivated/intoxicated by her love.*[43]

God created sex for pleasure and procreation in a marriage relationship between a man and a woman. That's the place and purpose of sex. I'm just saying what I see the Manual saying.

Every good manual contains warnings, often highlighted in big red letters. Misusing a product can have disastrous consequences, and limit its intended usefulness and blessing. It's the same with sex.

Misusing a product can have disastrous consequences

WARNINGS!

Here are a few warnings about sex from the Manual:

- *Avoid sexual immorality and fornication*[44]
- *Flee sexual immorality and fornication*[45]
- *Don't defraud or take advantage of one another*[46]

The Manual does not instruct you to "avoid sex", but it does warn you to *"avoid sexual immorality and fornication."* In the New Living Translation, it says it like this: *"God's will is for you to be holy, so stay away from all sexual sin."* In our secular humanistic culture, where relativism and existentialism rule the world, the very idea of sin – and especially sexual sin that relates to personal choices and actions – does not sit well. Sexual sin is definitely not a popular concept in our culture.

Throughout the Manual sin literally means "to miss the mark", like an arrow not hitting the target. But what is the target? What is the mark we are supposed to be aiming for? Well, it's not an arbitrary list of rules that God thought up on his day off to test you. Sin is anything that misses the mark of living in the image of God in which we were created. His image is the target, the standard. Sin is anything that is contrary to God's nature. Lying is a sin because God doesn't lie. So is stealing. Holiness is not being religious or good; it's being like God and living as he created you to live.

So what then is the sexual sin, or fornication, that the Manual warns us to avoid? Well, it's simply any sex outside of a marriage between a husband and wife. Of course, whether you accept this definition will depend on how much you accept the Manual as your guide. He also created you with a free will to make your choices, but unfortunately, you cannot choose the consequences of your choices.

Here's the 'why' of this warning in the Manual: *God's will is for you to be holy, so stay away from all sexual sin. Then each of you will control his own body and live in holiness and honour— not in lustful passion like those who do not know God and his ways.*[47]

From this, I submit to you today that God has a will and a way for your life, and when you choose his will and ways you will experience true life and relationship to the max. God's will is always good, pleasing and perfect.[48] The point is actually not virginity or purity, but holiness. Holy living is living whole. Holy living is happy living. Purity is a part of living holy. Purity never limits you. It protects you, and produces amazing blessings of freedom, wholeness, and security. Most people think that all the Manual says about sex is "avoid sex until marriage" – but that's just not true. Choosing God's will and way empowers you to get the very best out of the Maker's design for you, and that includes using your desires to live life to the max before marriage as well as in marriage.

There are two approaches to sex and sexuality: The passionate lust way, and the holy way. There's Hollywood sex, and there's holy sex, and I'll tell you what you want, what you really, really want is holy sex. You want it like God made it. You want the genuine thing. That's what the Manual prescribes. Anything else is counterfeit. It's cheating you. Hollywood sex will never satisfy. It's fine for lusting, but not for love.

In fact, the Manual goes even further by warning you to *"flee from sexual immorality"*[49] not just avoid it. Run from it. Like Joseph did, when Potiphar's wife asked him to sleep with her.[50] Joseph first *refused* (he wasn't confused about his values and what was right), then he *resisted* (because she asked again and again), and when she finally grabbed him, he *ran*. He left his coat behind and got outta there because a good run is better than a bad stand. If you find yourself in a condition of sin because you've put yourself in a position to sin, then I would suggest that it is time for you to run. Be willing to leave something behind, even if it costs you in the short term, it will be so worth it in the long term. Just ask Joseph. As they say, you can't stop the birds flying over your head, but you can stop them building a nest. Refuse. Resist. Run.

A good run is better than a bad stand

The Manual also says: *"each of you must control his own body and live in holiness and honour."*[51] Control sounds so limiting, doesn't it? But it's only limiting if you are confused about what you want and where you are going. If you look at the habits and skills of people who have had great visions for their lives · and seen those visions come to pass · then you will find they learnt how to exercise control and restraint. They had to learn how to say "no" to some choices, in order to say "yes" to others, that would lead them towards their goal. For those who don't know or care where they are going, any direction will do, but a clear vision of your future helps you decide your actions and choices today. A vision for a healthy, fulfilled relationship will empower you to say "no" to what you need to say "no" to, and "yes" to what is good and right and what will lead you to what you really, really want.

A Final Warning

"It is God's will that ... no-one should mistreat or take advantage of their brother or sister in this issue. The Lord punishes people for all these things, as we told you before and sternly warned you.[52]

It's not just about you. God expects your approach to sexuality and sex to take others into account too. Love always takes others into account, while lust only takes in order to satisfy self. Love gives for the benefit of others even at the expense of self, while lust always takes, to benefit self at the expense of others. Sex is not for lust; it's for love. It's for giving, not taking. Don't just think of yourself. God expects you to fully consider the person you are attracted to in all you think or do.

Here's a final word from the Manual:

Don't run roughshod over the concerns of your brothers and sisters. Their concerns are God's concerns, and he will take care of them. We've warned you about this before. God hasn't invited us into a disorderly, unkempt life but into something holy and beautiful—as beautiful on the inside as the outside.[53]

You have to decide: Do you believe the myths or the Manual?

My great prayer for you is that above the noise and distractions of the culture in which you find yourself, you will know the truth, believe it, and choose to follow it in faith, believing that God's way truly does lead to the life that you really, really want.

Now, let's look at what the Manual calls the "profound mystery" about sex. This may be one of the most revolutionary and radical things you'll hear about sex and marriage.

THE MYSTERY OF SEX

There is one great mystery about sex to understand: ALL SEX JOINS.

Through sex, two become one. Here's how the Manual puts it:

> For this reason a man will leave his father and mother and be united to his wife, and the two will become one flesh." This is a profound mystery - but I am talking about Christ and the church.[54]

> Don't you know that anyone who is joined to someone who is sleeping around is one body with that person? The scripture says, The two will become one flesh.[55]

The Message Translation says it like this:

There's more to sex than mere skin on skin. Sex is as much spiritual mystery as physical fact. As written in Scripture, "The two become one."[56]

To "become one flesh" literally means two people becoming fused together at the deepest level. Through all sex, there is a deep fusion between the two people involved. The mystery of sex is that this fusion is not just of two bodies, but something happens in the soul and the spirit as well. Of course, if this is true then it means that you really need to be sure that you want to be one with the one you are having sex with, and if you join yourself to someone that you don't really want to be one with, the result will be confusion rather than fusion.

All sex joins

Some Science on this Subject

But isn't sex just two bodies connecting for a little bit (or a lot) of fun? Let me share some science that shows the Manual is correct, and that all sex does indeed join. In a book called *Hooked: New Science on How Casual Sex is Affecting Our Children*,[57] a group of neuroscientists (neither Christians, nor having any religious agenda) record their findings from a fascinating study of the bonding mechanisms in the human brain. With regard to a female bonding chemical called Oxytocin, they found that "during sexual intercourse and orgasm, the woman's brain is flooded with Oxytocin, causing her to desire this same kind of contact again and again with this man she has bonded to, producing even stronger bonding." Men have a similar bonding chemical called Vasopressin, and their research showed that "when a male engages in sex, Vasopressin is released, bonding him to his partner and also stimulating the desire for more sex." They conclude that "there is evidence that when this sex/bonding/breakup cycle is repeated a few or many times – even when the bonding was short-lived – damage is done to the important built in ability to develop a significant and meaningful connection to other human beings." The Amazon book summary includes the following summary statements:

- Sexual activity releases chemicals in the brain, creating emotional bonds between partners.
- Breaking these bonds can cause depression and make it harder to bond with someone else in the future.

This research indicates that sex is not designed to be a part of the search for a partner. Sex with multiple partners actually confuses that search. It also clearly points to the fact that we were physically designed to have a committed, monogamous relationship in which sex is designed to fuse two people together ("two become one"). It seems to me that the Manual is right, and any assumption by our culture that there is no harm done in sleeping around during The Chase is simply not true and can actually cause lasting damage. One interviewee in the book sums it up like this: "I had no idea having sex as a teenager could affect the rest of my life."

Ok, that's the science done. Are you convinced that all sex joins?

Now let's look at two super important things you need to know about sex that will help you to understand what the Manual calls *the mystery of sex*. Firstly, that Biblical marriage is a blood covenant, and secondly, that sex is a covenant activity.

1. Biblical marriage is a blood covenant

I know that doesn't sound very sexy, but stay with me, ok? A covenant is a legal contract or agreement, but Biblical marriage is more than that. It's a blood covenant. This type of relationship was the most solemn and enduring contract between persons in the Hebrew tradition and was established not by a simple signing of a signature, but it always involved at least the following three elements:

- It brought the parties into complete unity and agreement · "what's mine is yours."
- It was to last forever · "until death parts us."
- It was always established by the flow of blood in some form.

There are a number of examples of blood covenants throughout the Old Testament of the Bible, but all these pointed to the ultimate blood covenant: Jesus' own death on the cross. In Ephesians 5:31·32 the apostle Paul speaks about the mystery of a man and woman coming together as one flesh in marriage as a picture of Jesus giving himself, his very life, for his bride, the church. As his blood flowed on the cross he gave his own sinless life for all sin that separates us from God, and he did away with every other covenant that ever had any claim on you.

You may be saying, "Yes, Wolfi, I get that, but how is marriage a blood covenant?" For a blood covenant there must be blood involved, so where's the blood in sex and marriage?

Well, let me give you a little biology lesson and show you a powerful reason why you should treasure your virginity and keep it for your marriage partner. This is important because I believe that understanding this mystery of sex is one of the most empowering truths regarding your sexuality.

So let's imagine it's the wedding day of a couple who are both virgins. Once the ceremony and celebration are over, the couple head off into the sunset to their honeymoon suite. That night when they express their love through sexual intercourse, as the man's penis penetrates his virgin wife's vagina for the first time, it has to break through a thin membrane called the hymen which stretches across a small part of the vaginal opening. Please note that the hymen can break before first sexual intercourse, during sports or other activities. But in cases where the hymen is still intact, it would tear and a small amount of blood flows onto the penis.[58] The purpose of the hymen still baffles evolutionary biologists today, because they can find no reason for its existence in the female body. I propose that God created a woman's hymen, and purposed for it to be a symbol of blood covenant in marriage. Wow! David the Psalmist had it exactly right when he declared:

"I will praise You, for I am fearfully and wonderfully made; Marvelous are your works, And that my soul knows very well."[59]

You could call this *the glory of virginity,* with glory meaning the magnificence, beauty, or weight of a thing. This understanding that marriage is a blood covenant, and the role of sex in that, gives huge weight to the reasoning that sex is worth keeping for the one person you marry. This gives you every reason to treasure your virginity and your sexual passions. Your virginity is part of the dowry you bring into your marriage to bless your life partner.

One more very important thing about virginity is that it is not just something for women to treasure, but also men. The blood flows over male and female, and it's a blood covenant for both. Consider that a male has two testicles, and that word carries the meaning of testifying or to be a witness. Guys, those two witness what you get up to, and let me just say, as bluntly as I can, you can't separate your testicles from your testimony!

Hey, I know this hasn't exactly been your usual glossy magazine sex story, but if you get this you will get freedom from all the junk and perversion associated with sex and sexuality. Jesus wants you to live free. Not by rules, but by the revelation of truth.

2. Sex is always a covenant activity

I know this doesn't sound very sexy, but stay with me because it will be worth it!

There is no such thing as casual sex, only covenant sex. Your sexual organs are covenant instruments. Sex is a powerful part of fusing two souls together as one in a marriage covenant. Just as sex can lead you into a holy

---

covenant it can lead you into an unholy covenant. While not all sex establishes a marriage covenant, there is a joining that takes place when you have sexual intercourse. In marriage, sex fuses the soul, but sexual immorality brings confusion to the soul, leading to what is often referred to as a "soul tie". A soul tie occurs when one person's soul gets "tied up" or enslaved to another person or multiple persons with whom you have had sexually immoral relations. This results in not having full possession of your mind, will and emotions.

There is no such thing as casual sex, only covenant sex

Imagine strings tied from your heart to every person with whom you have ever had immoral sexual relations, and all the strings pulling in different directions at different times. This is a picture of soul ties at work. You may find yourself saying, doing and thinking things you don't really want to, or staying with someone who you don't really like. You may even stay with or keep going back to physically or emotionally abusive partners. Your will is not free because you have tied yourself to another person or multiple persons through sexual immorality (because all sex joins). It's not just the physical act of intercourse that can cause a soul tie. Jesus made a radical claim that even looking at a woman lustfully is the same as committing adultery, so one would expect that pornography and sexual fantasies have much the same soul-confusing effect. If you personally struggle with porn, please find help urgently, because this will be a massive stumbling block to your ability to relate well. (Try www.xxxchurch.com · it's a helpful resource, providing encouragement and practical help for those wanting freedom in this area).

Soul ties are covenants which need to be acknowledged and then broken. There is one blood covenant which can supersede and break every other enslaving covenant in your life, and that is the one through the blood of Jesus Christ on the cross. There he announced that "It is finished" and with that released his power to set every captive free, and to restore every person to wholeness in soul, spirit and body. You too can experience this freedom through faith in Jesus. I'll help you do this in the final chapter.

Let me add something very important here: If you have given your virginity away and have had sexual relations with one or more people, then I want you to know and believe that God can make you whole in your soul and restore the glory of your virginity. This requires you to repent, believe, and receive. Repentance is not just being sorry for what you have done, and definitely not just being sorry for being caught or for the consequences of sin. Rather, it starts with a change of mind specifically about God and sin. You will struggle to turn from anything sinful until you believe that sin always deceives, destroys and disgraces, and that God is always good and his ways are best. These two convictions will empower you to turn away from sin and in faith towards God, and find him ready to forgive and restore you, and restore to you the glory of your virginity. Do this, and receive his forgiveness and restoration right now. There's no need to wait.

God has a heart full of compassion for those who have sinned sexually. Remember the Samaritan woman Jesus met at a well? She hadn't just messed up once - she'd had five husbands and was now shacking up with another guy. She had looked for love in the arms and beds of many men but found none. Now the man Jesus stands in front of her, and to her surprise, he doesn't condemn or reject her, but instead, he has gone out of his way to meet her and reveal his salvation to her. Through this encounter, she is totally changed. Where previously she was hiding in shame, going about her business at midday, when she was least likely to bump into anyone, she now rushes back to town and says to anyone who will listen to come and meet the man who knew everything she'd ever done (and everyone in the town knew she'd done a lot, with a lot of the men!).

If your sexual story is filled with any shame and regrets, remember that the blood covenant of Jesus can change everything for your future:

> *This means that anyone who belongs to Christ has become a new person.*
>
> *The old life is gone; a new life has begun!*[60]

Let your new life and living begin!

The DateTalk Truth:

All sex joins

Pause to think and talk about it:

- What one thing did you find most helpful or insightful in this chapter?

- Did anything in this chapter change the way you view sex? How?

- What is one thing that you will apply to your own relationship journey from this chapter?

Chapter Seven

THE HIGHWAY

In this chapter, we take a look at a better way to do this relationship journey that avoids the pitfalls and potholes of Lovers' Lane. I call this The HighWay.

Previously we saw that according to the Manual there are two ways to do relationships, either *"in a way that is holy and honourable"* or *"in lustful passion like those who do not know God and His ways."* To do something in an honourable way means that you place a high value on everything and everyone involved, including you, the other individual, and God. His ways are the best way to live and do relationships. They are not restrictive, boring, out-of-date, or prudish. Rather, they are life-giving, freeing, protective, and will lead you into the best life you can possibly experience. But you will need to walk this road in faith, believing The HighWay Promise, which I'll share in a moment. Trusting God and living by faith takes guts though because it requires that you lean on God in absolute trust, and confidence in his power, wisdom and goodness, in every area of your life.

Faith is the leaning of the whole human personality on God in absolute trust and confidence in His power, wisdom and goodness.

Most of us have messed up or have been messed up doing relationships our own way. Or maybe you have been too afraid or confused to even try. Is there a better way? How do we pursue relationships without hurting others and without getting hurt ourselves? How do we do the "two become one" journey well?

There are two things you need to know to travel The HighWay: The HighWay Promise and The HighWay Code.

THE HIGHWAY PROMISE

Jesus Himself made this HighWay Promise in Matthew 6:33 when he said, *"Seek first the Kingdom of God, and His righteousness, and all these things will be added to you."* The Message Translation puts it like this: *"Steep your life in God-reality, God-initiative, God-provisions. Don't worry about missing out. You'll find all your everyday human concerns will be met."* The HighWay Promise is simply this: you will find everything else you need and are looking for as you put your relationship with God first and fully trust him. Get on The HighWay, and there you will find what you want, what you really, really want. When you are on The HighWay, God will add, you don't have to grab.

On The HighWay, you are not seeking a boyfriend or girlfriend, you're seeking something greater: the Kingdom of God, which Jesus said is like a field a person buys in order to get the treasure that is buried there. You can't get your hands on the true treasure until you buy the whole field. Don't live for a few kisses, when you can have the whole Kingdom.

When you choose to live like this, your questions also change. No longer do you ask: "What are the rules?" or "How far can I go?" It's more: "How do I pursue a relationship with honour?" and "How do I conduct myself to ensure others don't get hurt in the process?" When this is at the heart of your journey, the boundaries you set for physical involvement and other priorities will be purpose driven, rather than just an exercise in suppressing your passion.

So, do you really believe The HighWay promise? Or would you rather travel your own way?

THE HIGHWAY CODE

If you have already passed your driver's test, you will know that there are special rules for driving on a highway (or motorway here where I live). These are needed because driving on a highway is usually faster and, therefore, potentially more risky. If all drivers know and obey the highway code, the benefits of a highway are great because it gets you to your destination faster than an ordinary road. This is also true for the relationship HighWay. If you are committed to travelling on The HighWay, then you will be open to learn and live by The HighWay Code. Without this, you will be a danger to others and yourself, and probably be the cause of a few painful accidents. So here's the code:

Code 1: Only lovers allowed

Code 2: Value fellow travellers

Code 3: Keep the right distance

Code 4: Change lanes carefully and clearly

Code 5: Get insurance

Code 6: No towing

Code 7: Observe the speed limit

Code 8: Obey the signs

Code 1: Only lovers allowed

Not everyone is qualified to drive on a highway. The HighWay is the love way, not a lust way. It's for lovers only, not lusters. You have to be careful of lusters taking their chances on The HighWay. They are dangerous because lusters care more about themselves than they do for others. Lovers care for others even at the expense of themselves. Lovers can have friends without creating the constant pressure to pair up. Lovers make The HighWay a safe place to travel, but lusters should be banned. Decide to be a lover, not a luster.

Code 2: Value your fellow travellers

It's not just about you, and your happiness. God loves and values every person as much as he loves and values you. He loves every other person and they belong to him first, and he expects you to treat others as having high value. Also, some of your fellow travellers are not dating options for you, because they already belong to someone else. To break this code is cheating, or at worst adultery. Do not commit adultery. Don't defraud others along the way. Value your fellow travellers highly.

Code 3: Keep the right distance

When driving on a highway, you will often notice signs to remind you to keep a safe distance between you and the vehicle in front of you. Being too close to another car when you are driving at speed and suddenly need to react to something going wrong can have disastrous consequences. It's the same with relationships, where keeping the right distance both physically and emotionally can be the making or breaking of a relationship. Think about distance as having healthy boundaries. Boundaries are not there to restrict you, but to allow you to keep what you don't want out, and keep what you do want in. It is your responsibility to regulate not only your physical but also your emotional boundaries. The basic guideline is that your level of emotional intimacy with someone of the opposite sex should not exceed your level of commitment to each other. When you share intimate personal feelings and thoughts with someone that you don't share with many others, you are giving them privileged access to your heart. Keeping a safe distance on The

HighWay means being careful to open up beyond the level of commitment. As much as you like them and you think that they are trustworthy, there are certain deep parts of you to which someone must earn access through commitment. This is particularly true if the other person is not single, but showing interest in you. If they are single, and you feel some "wow", then proceed with caution and in proportion to the commitment they are showing to your friendship and relationship.

Code 4: Change lanes carefully and clearly

When driving on a highway it is not safe to go swerving randomly from one lane to another. And when you do want to change lanes, it's important to indicate clearly so everyone knows your intentions. Some people do the relationship journey like a guy who is driving along and has forgotten to switch off his indicator and no one knows when or where he intends to turn. Others are like a car I used to have which just would not drive straight but always had a veer to the left. It just wouldn't stay in its lane. Those types are dangerous on a highway.

It's the same on the relationship HighWay. There is a time to stay in your own lane, and there is a time to merge with someone else's lane, but don't go swerving all over the place. To travel safely on The HighWay you need to learn to communicate your feelings and intentions clearly and confidently. Don't leave the others guessing. "He loves me, he loves me not" is not a game for The HighWay. And if you do come across someone swerving all over the place, or not indicating clearly, you would do well to recommend that they go and read DateTalk chapter two on what it means to be a whole one.

Code 5: Get insurance

Love is always a risk, and when there is no risk of some heartbreak, then it's probably not love you're involved with. You should never travel on the relationship journey without insurance because sometimes things don't work out as you want them to, and accidents happen: rejection, misunderstanding, breakup, etc. When you do have an accident, it's good to have some insurance in place.

Your friends and family are the best insurance you can have while you are on a relationship journey. Don't cut them off. Let a few people into the secret parts of your life. Give someone the right to ask you the difficult questions. Don't let your insurance expire because you are too focused on the one you are pursuing, but keep investing in relationship with friends and family. They are the ones who will be there for you if things go wrong. Don't wait until an accident happens and then try to find insurance. It doesn't work that way in real life, and it's not good practice on The HighWay either.

Code 6: No towing

Travelling on The HighWay is every person's individual choice, so don't try to drag someone along with you. I personally don't recommend mission dating, which is dating someone who has beliefs or core values vastly different to yours, with the hope that you will change them to believe and think like you. There have been some exceptions that have worked out, but my advice is that you should generally assume that you are not the exception. Trust me, towing on a highway is really tricky and the same can be said for dragging someone along the relationship HighWay against their will. So no towing recommended.

Code 7: Observe the speed limit

Speed can kill. There is a speed limit on The HighWay; too fast too soon is dangerous, and it usually means that Eros is in the driving seat of the relationship. On The HighWay, there is also a minimum speed: don't drag your exclusive relationship out over years and years, keeping the other guessing about when you may be ready for a marriage commitment. Patience belongs on The HighWay because it is the first characteristic of love, but procrastination and double-mindedness do not.

Code 8: Obey the signs

There are signs on a highway that you need to obey to avoid danger: STOP. SLOW DOWN. BEWARE. The signs in a relationship are not always as clear as those on a highway, but there are some obvious clues that should help you interpret that there is danger or disappointment ahead:

- A one-sided relationship · where it consistently seems one person is doing all the giving, and the other is doing all the taking.
- Lies · perhaps small ones at first, where it becomes easier to dodge around some issue than to talk honestly about it.

- Manipulation · where someone feels they have to manoeuvre their partner to get what they want, rather than talking about their needs.

- Compromise · where one person starts to feel they cannot be truly themselves, holding to their own core values, because of what their partner may think, or because of fears the relationship will end as a result.

- Violation of your stated boundaries · where one person feels they are being pushed beyond what they are comfortable with emotionally or physically in the relationship.

- Controlling · where one person starts to demand their partner conform to their expectations.

- Devaluation, where a person starts to use negative words or sarcasm to their partner · even in jest at first · which could lead to more serious verbal abuse, or more.

When these things are part of any relationship you are in, then put your indicator on and get out of that lane quickly. You need to realise that you have somehow merged lanes with someone who is not a whole one, so STOP. SLOW DOWN. BEWARE. If you don't, you're heading down Lovers' Lane, and into a ditch.

THE HIGHWAY JOURNEY

It is my desire that DateTalk will get you on The Highway or help you stay on it, and that you will enjoy and complete the journey in God's good time. A typical journey on The HighWay to a fulfilled relationship follows a pattern:

It starts with a whole you

Acquaintance

Friendship

WOW, WOw, Wow, wow, woW, wOW or mmm...

Courtship

I do, or I don't

Let's look at each of these.

A whole you

The HighWay journey to a fulfilled relationship begins with you being committed to personal wholeness, becoming the person that the person you are looking for is looking for. Check out chapter one again, and commit yourself to personal wholeness, because that's the best preparation you can make for a future fulfilled relationship.

Acquaintance

This is the meeting new people part of the journey. This is not like The Chase of Lovers' Lane, where the motivation is all focussed on pairing up and meeting that someone special to make you feel special. Meeting new people is just a healthy way of doing life. All sorts of different people in different kinds of places: at school, uni, college, work, play, parties, socials, church, hobbies, sport, doing charity work, at weddings, etc. Some of this may also happen on social media or dating sites. Acquaintances are those you rub shoulders with as you do life, but they are not necessarily going to the same destination as you, in the same direction as you, or at the same pace as you.

Friendship

On this part of the journey, you recognise that some people in the crowd are actually going in the same direction as you. Some a little slower, some a little faster. Some married, some single, some divorced, some old, some young, some yellow, some pink, some chocolate, some rich, some poor, some tall, some short, some male, some female, some men, some women – a wonderful mix of interesting and amazing human beings. They don't necessarily share all your views or values, but what makes them special is that they are generally travelling in a similar direction to you in some area of life. This is a great discovery: friends. Life becomes richer with them.

What makes this a great part of The HighWay journey is that there is a positive atmosphere with no pressure to be dating someone special and to have a boy/girlfriend. It's an environment where you can build friendships without pressure, in a group situation. Here we can be ourselves, and we can get to know one another without pretence. Can I make an appeal to all my fellow Christians? Let's be committed to creating these kind of friendship environments in our church communities. This means no stupid comments and questions like: "Who's your boyfriend?" or "What's someone like you still doing on your own?" or "When are you going to find someone?" or "I thought you would be married by now." NO! Make a decision and agree that in your circle of friendship and church community you will have attitudes and create environments that respect everyone, with equal sensitivity to the needs of both single and married people.

The benefits of getting to know people in a friendship environment are huge. In friendship, we serve together, and the way he serves others will show you how he will serve you. In friendship, we support each other, and the way she supports others will show how she will support you. In friendship, we honestly share ideas and feelings together, and the way someone opens up will reveal how they will be in a relationship. In friendship, it's not "Try before you buy" like in the typical dating pattern. Friendship is a safe place to get to know the real person. Friendship recognises that you don't discover the real person by exploring their body in the dark!

Friendship is a safe place to get to know the real person

A last important note about friendship. Please don't make a big deal or be paranoid about spending time alone with a friend now and again as you begin to discover common interests or attractions. Some alone time is a nice and necessary part of getting to know someone better. Just keep The HighWay code and you'll be safe as you move into the next exciting part of The HighWay journey, which I call the "wow" stage.

WOW, WOw, Wow, wow, woW, wOW or mmm

There are lots of varieties of "wow". So here's how it's going: You are on The HighWay with friends who are largely going in the same direction as you. You're advancing. You're not cruising and choosing, or trying before you're buying. You are living by faith in The HighWay Promise, positioned to have all you need added to you in God's good time. Now you are ready for what I call the "wow" stage. Let me describe this part of the journey:

People behind and ahead of you. Friends going in a similar direction. Some advancing faster, some slower. You're liking some more than others. Then you notice someone who is travelling this road with you. Like Adam, who woke up one morning and there she was, and all he could say was "WO(W)man!" Or maybe it's not that dramatic. You start to notice and feel attracted to someone you've known for a while, and it's a "wow" (Not quite a WOW!). Or maybe you've known someone for years, and it's more like a "mmm." Something you haven't noticed before catches your attention and attracts you and makes your heart beat a little or a lot faster. Whether it happens as "WOW, WOw, Wow, wow, woW, wOW or mmm," it's all the same thing. It's natural. It's exciting. It's powerful and can be quite dangerous. That's why you need to have your HighWay code well programmed into your brain before this happens because this will help you make sure you have the right criteria for the wow factor. The Wisdom Book of Proverbs says that "Beauty and charm are deceitful, but a woman who fears the Lord, she is to be praised".[61] You need to programme that in now because some wow factors will override any half-hearted commitment to The HighWay code. Guys and girls have different challenges to overcome when the wow factor kicks in. Remember guys are often initially attracted by sight, so what they see can often override what they think and know and believe. For girls, what they feel can often override straight-thinking when the wow factor kicks in for them.

It's at this stage that you urgently need your insurance in place as you figure out what to do with the WOW, WOw, Wow, wow, woW, wOW or mmm that is coming over you.

Courtship

I know that courtship doesn't sound like a very sexy response to wow, but if you get this right it will hugely help you navigate through your WOW, WOw, Wow, wow, woW, wOW or mmm in the best possible way. So what is it? Well, courtship is a mature response to when you feel the wow for someone. It's an attitude that says, "Help!" I need help to do relationship well. I need help to choose my helper well. It's a recognition that love · the love that you are feeling · is potentially blind or at least blinkered, and that you need others to help you to see clearly as you move forward in your pursuit of this blossoming relationship. Why? Well, because the beginning of WOW, WOw, Wow, wow, woW, wOW or mmm is often very emotional (If it isn't, then you probably need some help anyway). Feelings are not wrong or right, they just are. Emotions make wonderful servants, but lousy masters, and healthy courtship helps you keep emotions serving you, rather than ruling and potentially ruining you and your blossoming relationship. Courtship is not a programme or method or law, but rather a healthy way to process your feelings. It includes at least three parts: God, your Court, and sharing your feelings with the wow person.

Emotions make wonderful servants, but lousy masters

Get God involved

God is the great Matchmaker. He is still in the joining together business. He still leads and guides. He knows everything. He sees the end from what you feel is the beginning. Get him involved big time. Trust him. Talk to him. Honour him. Let him guide you in all sorts of ways. Keep confident faith in the great HighWay Promise.

Go to your Court

A mature person realises that there is wisdom in the counsel of many.[62] Take the initiative and ask for help and insights from trusted people who you know care for you and have your best interests at heart. Friends, Pastors, Counsellors, Parents. Make yourself accountable to some specific people. Share your feelings with one or two in your Court. Make sure that your insurance is up to date and that you are covered in case of an accident. You can also strengthen and add to your Court through reading good books and watching/listening to good teaching about various aspects of relationships. You're strengthening your Court by reading this book. Learning from others who have gone where you want to go is always a wise and helpful thing to do in any new endeavour.

Share your feelings and intentions clearly with your wow person

This is often a very tricky part. There comes a time to communicate what you are feeling. As a teenager falling in love, I was useless at this. I didn't say what I wanted to say and often did say what I never intended to say. It was a disaster! My actions often spoke much louder than my words, and that was seriously confusing.

Don't communicate what you don't mean. Guys, if you're going to say "I love you" then make sure you mean it, and you're not just verbalising something from your depleted right brain because you are experiencing some BRP effects!

Talking about guys, should the guy always make the first move, or can the girl also take the initiative? I personally don't see what's wrong with either, as long as both move towards a point of mutual commitment and understanding, after that first "initiation" has happened. I do think that guys generally prefer to be the hunter than to be hunted. It's just something about our manhood. Men that are pursued too strongly often run away, not necessarily because they don't like the girl, but simply because they don't feel comfortable with that approach. Traditionally, men are said to fear commitment too, which can make them reluctant to take the step and initiate. Many guys also suffer from serious passivity because of a fear of failure. You will have to deal with these fears sooner of later, so if any of this is a struggle for you, go back and get your Court involved for some wisdom and encouragement.

Wild at Heart by John Eldredge for guys, and *Captivating* by John and Stasi Eldredge for girls are insightful reads. *Wild at Heart* describes three core desires of men: to fight a courageous battle, to live a great adventure, and to rescue a beauty. *Captivating* describes three core desires for women: to be romanced, to play an irreplaceable role in a great adventure, and to unveil beauty. Many thousands of men and women have found these books helpful in discovering who they are, or explaining why they feel the way they do about parts of their lives.

Remember: Courtship is about getting to know the real person. It's about seeing the big picture. Be careful of short circuiting this by getting distracted by physical involvement. In marriage preparation, we ask a question: "If you could do it over again, what would you do differently?" Most often couples reply: "We would slow down on physical intimacy." Avoid the catalysts for Eros, and no hormone racing exercises on couches – and definitely no sleepovers. Save that for the big day and beyond. Spend your time doing things together.

Courtship is about getting to know the real person

Get to know each other's friends (you can tell a lot about a person by their friends, or lack of them). Don't just merge everything straight away. Stay separately involved with and connected to your friends, and your commitments to people and places and causes.

I do, or I don't

The Courtship part of the journey helps you figure out whether the one you have WOW, WOw, Wow, wow, woW, wOW or mmm feelings for is really the one with whom you want to spend the rest of your life. This is a massive decision, and one you definitely do not want to make flippantly. Courtship should help you get to a place of confidence that this is the person you want to say "I do" to. Or to realise that you'd missed something important and this is not the relationship for you. Courtship should be open to both outcomes, otherwise you might as well skip this stage.

Please, please note that your Court is only there to help you make the decision, not to make the decision for you. You are also not asking for permission. You are ultimately the one who decides and chooses. If this goes all the way to the wedding altar you will have full responsibility for saying "I do." You can't say, "My mother thinks I should marry him," or, "My friends like him," or even, "God told me to." You need to take full responsibility for your decision as you say "I DO."

If courtship leads you to an "I don't" decision, then that's ok. That's good for you, and good for the other person. Better no man than the wrong man. Better no woman than the wrong woman. Better a bit of short term pain and disappointment and dented ego, than a lifetime of it. Who you commit to spending the rest of your married life with is the biggest decision you will ever make (besides what you believe about God).

Remember, marriage is the goal, not just a wedding. Marriage is for life, not just for the wedding day and night. Sex will be great, but sooner or later it will usually produce children. Children are a great blessing in a marriage, but also require a solid dose of commitment. He will be the father of your children. They will call her mother. This will go on through sickness and in health, for better or for worse, for richer or for poorer, until death parts you. When you are sure that that's what you really want with someone, then go ahead and say, "I do."

So there you have it, The HighWay journey. What I have described is certainly not the only way to get to "I do", and many have taken other routes and got to the destination of a fulfilled relationship. But many more have taken other routes and detours and sadly never reached their desired destination. Instead, they ended up with disappointment, heartache, hurt, disillusionment, hopelessness, loneliness, soul ties, and sadly also divorce. I hope you will believe The HighWay Promise, and commit yourself to doing it The HighWay.

The DateTalk Truth:

On the HighWay you will find what you want, what you really, really want

Pause to think and talk about it:

- What one thing did you find most helpful or insightful in this chapter?

Consider the following questions to evaluate how your personal relationship journey to date compares to The HighWay:

- What is similar, and what is different?

- What do you agree with?

- What, if anything, do you disagree with, and why?

- What's the most important thing you need to do or think about differently?

- What is one thing that you will apply to your own relationship journey from this chapter?

Chapter Eight

RECALCULATING YOUR WAY FORWARD

Have you ever been in a car when the driver is following directions on a sat nav system and they take a turn that is different to the suggested route? This is when the satnav lady (Why is it always a woman's voice giving the directions?) announces that the satnav is "recalculating". It's still got the desired destination programmed into it but is now going to give you new directions and suggest a new way to get to the same destination. This works, as long as you keep the original destination programmed into the system.

It's the same with relationships. Most of us set out to find a healthy, happy and fulfilled relationship, but often lose our way by taking one or more wrong turns. If this is where you are at, then it's time to recalculate and get back on track to get to your goal.

One reality of life is that you will never change direction or be committed to a new direction unless you are convinced that the way you were going is ultimately going to leave you empty and broken. Deep inside you, there must arise a solid conviction that there is a better way to do relationships. You must become convinced that the way of passionate lust is not the way you want to go, and you must deeply reject this kind of living and start to yearn for a better way. Like the prodigal son in the famous story Jesus told, you have to come to your senses to realise that the choices you have made and are making are leading you to the pigsty of life. Something has to change in your heart. Recalculating or "repentance" begins with a change of mind, and leads to a change of direction.

Deep inside you, there must arise a solid conviction that there is a better way to do relationships

For some of you that has happened in various places as you were reading this book. You may be hurting and even hopeless, but you know that God is inviting you to recalculate and commit yourself to seeking and walking in the ways he has begun to show you through these DateTalk truths. The great thing about Jesus is that he is "the way" and that through him you can always find the way back to the best of relationships and life. God has a good plan for your life and a new way for you to walk in that plan. It just requires you to want it, to turn from other ways to his ways, and follow him in faith.

If you are ready to do that, a helpful way to express yourself to God may be to pray the prayer that King David of old prayed right at the end of Psalm 139 to recommit himself to The HighWay, in a time when he himself had lost his way in a disastrous relationship decision:

Search me, O God, and know my heart;

Try me, and know my anxieties. See if there is any wicked way in me,

And lead me in the way everlasting.

As we come to the end of our DateTalk journey, it's been my privilege to share with you (almost) everything you need to know about relations, dating, and sex! I do hope that it has given you some markers to help you chart your way forward into a new, exciting and fulfilled HighWay love story. Enjoy it, and may God richly bless you in this and every area of your life.

I bless your future with all of God's very best for your good and for his glory. May you continue to grow in loving well, and grow in knowing his great love for you in Jesus Christ.

Always remember: To love well is to live well.

The Final DateTalk Truth:

To love well is to live well

Pause to think and talk about it:

- What was the one most significant or helpful insight you have got out of the DateTalk book?

- What is one thing you will commit yourself to doing as a result of reading this book?

ENDNOTES

1   Story adapted from The Good Night Kiss, by Pastor Tim, 2003

2   Proverbs 13:12

3   John 4:7-30

4   John 8:1-11

5   Photo by Furman S. Baldwin, 1947, *Il Bacio* (The Kiss)

6   Modified from an internet circulated email.

7   Luke 15:11

8   Matthew 19:3

9   Matthew 19:4-6

10   John 8:32

11   John 14:6

12   Proverbs 4:20-22, NLT

13   Ephesians 2:10

14   Jeremiah 1:5

15   Psalm 139:14

16   Men Are from Mars, Women Are from Venus, John
      Gray, 1992

17   Rick Warren, *The Purpose Driven Life*, 2002,

18   Romans 12:2

19   2 Corinthians 10:12

20   John 3:16

21   John 15:13

22   Psalm 16:11

23   Matthew 19:5

24   Ecclesiastes 3:11

25   John 8:1-11

26   John 4

27   Luke 7:36-50

28   Matthew 19:4

29   Men Are from Mars, Women Are from Venus, John
      Gray, 1992

30   Ecclesiastes 8:15

31   Genesis 1:27

32   The Ten Commandments of Dating, Ben Young, Samuel Adams

33   Song of Solomon 2:5-6

34   Ecclesiastes 3:11

35   Genesis 1:28

36   Genesis 2:25

37   Genesis 4:1

38   Hebrews 13:4

39   Genesis 2:24

40   Genesis 4:1

41   2 Samuel 11

42   Hebrews 13:4

43   Proverbs 5:19

44   1 Thessalonians 4:3-8

45   1 Corinthians 6:18

46   1 Thessalonians 4:6

47   1 Thessalonians 4:3-5

48   Romans 12:2

49   1 Corinthians 6:18

50   Genesis chapter 39

51   1 Thessalonians 4:3-5

52   1 Thessalonians 4:6

53   1 Thessalonians 4:6-7 (MSG)

54   Ephesians 5:31, 32

55   1 Corinthians 6:16

56   1 Corinthians 6:16 (MSG)

57   Hooked, 2008, by Joe S. McIlhaney Jr. and Freda McKissic Bush.

58   No blood flowing in the marriage bed does not negate the blood covenant. The principle still stands because the Lord looks at the intentions of the heart, not the external details of things.

59   Psalm 139:14

60   2 Corinthians 5:17

61   Proverbs 31:30

62   Proverbs 15:22

THANK YOU'S

Thank you to all the fantastic single people who have over many years attended a DateTalk event and encouraged me to keep sharing the love.

Thank you to all those who have kept encouraging me to write. I said I'd get it done by Christmas. I just didn't say which Christmas!

Thank you to Abi Le Fevre, Aiden Beck, and a bunch of amazing other young singles who gave such helpful feedback to the early draft. You saved the book from a lot of cheese! (I did leave a bit just for good taste.)

A special thank you to Jo Chee and Wes Hinsley, for your very constructive feedback, input and suggestions. Your passion for getting this book out inspired me.

Thank you to my daughter Amy for working with me to design a unique book cover. And if you were one of the hundred's of people who commented on social media with your opinions about the cover design - thank you too. (We hope you love this one!)

Thank you to Fiona Matier, for your meticulous proofreading and final touches giving me the confidence to say it's done.

Thank you to I Am Self-Publishing for the typesetting design, and being willing to race against time to make the publishing deadline.

A massive thank you to my wife Ali, the love of my life, for loving me enough to allow me to learn to grow in loving well. And for always keeping me real. You're amazing!

Thank you to my God, who first loved me.

ABOUT THE AUTHOR

Wolfgang, or as he is affectionately known, Wolfi, is together with his wife the founding leader of Every Nation Church London. He also fulfils a strategic leadership role among the Every Nation churches in Europe and internationally. He and Ali have two daughters.

Born in Namibia with German as his home language, he grew up in South Africa. He was not raised in a Christian home but became a Christ follower in his late teens. After university and working as a project manager for a large construction company, his life took a new trajectory as he answered a call to vocational ministry. This led him and Ali to hear God's call to start a new church in London, and in 1993, having never been there before, and knowing no-one, they landed at Heathrow Airport with their "two backpacks and a vision". It's been an incredible adventure touching countless lives and nations through church planting, campus ministry and a passion to see the good news of God's amazing grace experienced by every person, and God's Kingdom come in every sphere of society.

Back in his youth he once ran a sub-four minute mile and has completed a couple of London marathons, but nowadays he prefers "board" meetings – especially snowboard and stand up paddleboard meetings!

RESOURCES & CONNECT

BOOKS

- "THE ART OF LOVING WELL", a book covering "*Ten powerful ways to change your relational climate*" (Available on Amazon and various retailers)
- "The Follow Course", an intentional three-part journey to help you grow as a follower of Jesus.

ONLINE

- Blog: www.wolfinlondon.com
- Church Website: www.everynation.london
- On my YouTube channel watch the "DateTalk" series for free via 6x28 minute videos and many other teachings.
- Other social media via whatever is current when you read this!

TV

- On www.tbnuk.org watch "The Art of Loving Well" programming as scheduled or via on-demand.

Remember:

To love well is to live well